Project YOU

MORE THAN 50 WAYS TO CALM DOWN, DE-STRESS, & FEEL GREAT!

AUBRE ANDRUS

with Karen Bluth, PhD

illustrations by Veronica Collignon

SWITCH
PRESS
a capstone imprint

Table of Contents

How to Use This Book

Cheerful! Energetic! Capable! Satisfied! Wouldn't you love to feel that way right now? With this book, you can. Really. Because even when you're feeling the exact opposite — tired, stressed out, or frustrated — you can totally transform your mindset and your emotions. Inside this book, you'll find activities, exercises, crafts, and recipes that can help you:

CALM YOUR ANXIETIES

OVERCOME THAT OVERWHELMED FEELING

FIND INSPIRATION

TAKE CONTROL OF NERVES

FEEL CONFIDENT

ACCOMPLISH YOUR GOALS

BURST INTO LAUGHTER

. . . AND GENERALLY *feel great.*

When you're having a rough day, doing something – *anything* – can make you feel better. It can be hard to get off the couch on one of those days. But it's amazing what can happen after you take that first step.

Flip through the pages of this book and choose the idea that piques your interest right now. There's no wrong or right answer, and no true beginning or end. The most important thing is that you do something to bust those bad feelings.

However, you can't use this book to solve serious mental health problems such as anxiety disorders, depression, or eating disorders. If at any point you think you need more help than this book can offer, please turn to page 154.

Wellness Check

A healthy mind and body includes a mix of many different things. Take inventory of where you stand. How many of these items can you already check off?

☐ I CAN MAKE AND KEEP FRIENDS.

☐ I TAKE ON CHALLENGES CONFIDENTLY.

☐ I OPEN MY MIND TO NEW IDEAS AND EXPERIENCES.

☐ I GET ALONG WELL WITH MY FAMILY MEMBERS.

☐ I HAVE CONTROL OVER MY FEELINGS.

☐ I DO NOT LET FEAR OR STRESS HOLD ME BACK.

☐ I ENJOY BEING ACTIVE.

☐ I ACCEPT FAILURE AND MOVE ON AFTER IT HAPPENS.

☐ I CALMLY EXPRESS ANGER AND FRUSTRATION.

☐ I TRY NOT TO COMPARE MYSELF TO OTHERS.

☐ I CAN MAINTAIN A BALANCED SCHEDULE.

☐ I SHARE MY THOUGHTS AND FEELINGS WITH PEOPLE I TRUST.

☐ I TRY TO APPRECIATE THE LITTLE THINGS.

☐ I EAT HEALTHY, ENERGIZING MEALS.

☐ I GET ENOUGH SLEEP EVERY NIGHT.

☐ I AM ABLE TO SHARE IN OTHERS' HAPPINESS.

☐ I CAN FORGIVE OTHERS AND MYSELF.

☐ I MAKE TIME TO RELAX AND DE-STRESS EVERY DAY.

☐ I FEEL STRONG BOTH INSIDE AND OUT.

☐ I SET GOALS AND WORK TOWARD THEM.

☐ I TRY NOT TO BE TOO HARD ON MYSELF.

☐ I FEEL ENERGIZED THROUGHOUT THE DAY.

☐ I HAVE A SENSE OF PURPOSE.

Take Control

Your first task? Find a solution that will help you set out on a path toward relaxation, peace of mind, and happiness. The following pages are filled with activities, exercises, advice, prompts, crafts, playlists, and recipes that can help you get there.

These do-right-now projects can help you manage your time, become more productive, and can help motivate you to try something new. Flip through the pages and choose the project that speaks to you most in this moment. If that exercise doesn't do the trick, try something else!

IF YOU STRUGGLE WITH STAGE FRIGHT OR PUBLIC
SPEAKING MAKES YOU SQUIRM → TRY THE BREATHING EXERCISES ON PAGE 20.

IF YOU'RE FREAKING OUT ABOUT
TOMORROW'S TEST → TRY THE PROGRESSIVE MUSCLE RELAXATION ON PAGE 56.

IF YOU'RE FEELING FED UP → TRY THE LOVING-KINDNESS MEDITATION ON PAGE 80.

IF YOU'RE SO WORRIED THAT YOU CAN'T
FALL ASLEEP → FOLLOW THE 60-MINUTE WIND-DOWN ON PAGE 140.

IF YOU'RE COMPLETELY UNORGANIZED → TRY TO PREPARE BETTER WITH THE TIPS ON PAGE 62.

IF YOU CAN'T DECIDE BETWEEN TWO THINGS → TRY THE DECISION-MAKING TIPS ON PAGE 146.

IF YOU'RE UNSURE OF YOUR FUTURE → LEARN HOW TO MAKE A VISION BOARD ON PAGE 114.

IF YOU'RE FEELING SELF-CONSCIOUS OR JEALOUS → TURN TO "STOP COMPARING" ON PAGE 150.

IF YOU CAN'T FIND ANYTHING IN YOUR BEDROOM → TURN TO PAGE 50 FOR ORGANIZATION TIPS.

IF YOUR WHOLE BODY FEELS TENSE → TURN TO PAGE 36 FOR MASSAGES YOU CAN GIVE YOURSELF.

IF YOU FEEL LIKE YOU'RE LACKING
A PURPOSE → LEARN MORE ABOUT VOLUNTEER OPPORTUNITIES ON PAGE 102.

IF YOU'RE FEELING DRAINED → LISTEN TO THE UPLIFTING MUSIC ON PAGE 82.

IF YOU HATE EVERYTHING IN YOUR CLOSET → LEARN HOW TO SIMPLIFY ON PAGE 52.

IF YOU'RE TOTALLY OVERWHELMED → LEARN HOW TO MEDITATE ON PAGE 8.

IF YOU'RE AFRAID TO STAND OUT → LEARN HOW TO IMPROVE YOUR POSTURE ON PAGE 122.

IF YOU'RE FEELING STUCK → TRY A 30-DAY CHALLENGE ON PAGE 116.

Meditate

Breath awareness is a core formal mindfulness practice. It is called a formal practice because you set aside time to do it every day. Start with 5 minutes and then add a few minutes each day until you're practicing for 20 minutes or more.

You use your breath in this practice as an anchor to the present moment because it's easy — you always have it with you. Breath and other physical sensations always exist in the present moment. Through feeling the sensation of your breath, you're training your mind to be in the present.

- First, find a comfortable place to sit. This can be on a cushion on the floor, or on a chair or couch. If you're sitting on a chair or couch, sit so that your feet are flat on the floor and you're sitting toward the front of the surface and not leaning against the back. Your hands can be relaxed in your lap or on your thighs — whatever is most comfortable for you. Check to make sure your shoulders are relaxed and not hunched. Your eyes can be open or closed. If they're open, keep your lids slightly lowered, and pick a place a few feet in front of you on the floor to rest your gaze.

The important thing is that you're sitting in a position where you can be alert. Mindfulness is about observing our moment to moment experience, and if we're not aware and alert, we can't do that. We'll just drift away into our thoughts.

- Now bring your attention to your breath in the place where you can most easily notice it. This might be at the tip of your nose as you're breathing in, or at your lips as you're breathing out through your mouth, or it might be in the slight rising and falling of your chest as you breathe, or maybe even in your diaphragm area just under your rib cage.

- Feel your breath as you breathe in and as you breathe out. See if you can feel your breath from the very beginning of your in-breath to the very end of your out-breath, even noticing the place where your in-breath turns into your out-breath. Notice the movement of your breath, the temperature of your breath, and maybe even the texture of your breath.

- Do this for each breath, noticing how each breath rises and falls away and noticing the space in between breaths.

- You'll soon be aware that your mind has drifted and you're thinking about something. When you notice this, simply direct your attention back to your breath. No need to judge yourself or feel like you're a "bad meditator." This is what the mind does: it wanders.

- Continue doing this — feeling your breath, noticing that your mind has wandered, and gently guiding your attention back to your breath. Think of your breath like a puppy on a leash. The puppy runs off, and you gently guide it back with the leash. It soon runs off again, and once again you gently guide it back.

That's it! Pretty simple, right? When you are in the moment, you are not dwelling on something that happened in the past or worrying about something that might happen in the future. Research has shown that when our minds wander, they tend to go to these places of worry and regret. So by gently guiding your attention back to the present moment, through paying attention to physical sensations like your breath, you are letting go of the thought processes that cause stress.

Everyday Mindfulness Practice

Mindfulness is about being in the present moment with an attitude of curiosity and without judgment. In other words, noticing what you're doing as you're doing it. Since physical sensations (hearing, seeing, touching, smelling, tasting) always take place in the present moment, physical sensations can bring you to the present moment. The more you stay in the present moment, the more you'll let go of stressing about things that may happen in the future or things you might regret about the past. This is why a lot of research has shown that people who practice mindfulness are less depressed, less anxious, and less stressed.

There are many ways that you can practice mindfulness "informally" during your day. You can practice mindfulness at any time: while you're walking to class, talking with friends, or playing sports. Here you will find a few examples of in-the-moment mindfulness practices.

ON YOUR WAY TO SCHOOL

This is a good practice to do if you're riding (not driving!) in a car or bus or even walking out in nature. Pay attention to sounds that you hear. Notice sounds that are nearby and sounds that are far away. Notice how they may fade in and then fade away. See how many different sounds you can hear. • • • • • • • • • •

Take a minute or two to just listen.

WHEN YOU'RE HAVING LUNCH

Eating is a great time to be mindful! As you are about to take a bite of an apple or raise a potato chip to your mouth, first notice the feeling of the food in your hand. Is it heavy? Light? Smooth? Rough? As you bring the food to your lips, notice if there's an aroma coming from the food. Sometimes it can be very strong, and other times it is subtle. When you bring the food to your lips and take a bite, notice all the sensations in your mouth. Sweet? Salty? Juicy? As you slowly chew, pay attention to the multitude of sensations that are present in your mouth. Notice when that one bite eventually dissolves and is gone. How does it feel in your mouth at that point? Now take another bite, paying attention to the same sensations.

DURING AN ARGUMENT

This practice is very helpful when you feel yourself getting upset. Immediately bring your attention to any place where your body has contact with something solid like the floor, a chair, or a table. Notice the feeling of your feet on the floor, your legs against the chair, or your hand on the table. Investigate what those physical sensations are like. Is the table cold to your touch? Is the chair hard? You can even bring your awareness to your breath and pay attention to the sensations of your in-breath and out-breath for several slow breaths. This will help keep you in the present and de-escalate any rising negative emotions.

Strike a (Yoga) Pose

Yoga is about calming your mind and your body. It's a series of poses that involve stretching, balancing, or relaxing. When you're tense, your muscles are tense too. Yoga can help relieve that pressure.

When trying a new pose, focus on your breathing as you move. Don't hold your breath! You can do these poses as a series, one after another, or you can just try one pose when you want to relax. Hold each pose for 30 seconds to one minute.

YOU WILL NEED:

a yoga mat
a comfortable outfit

Triangle Pose

Sanskrit name: Utthita Trikonasana

Step your right foot forward, toes pointing forward. Turn your left foot to a 90-degree angle. Turn your torso sideways. Lift your arms so they are parallel to the ground and in line with your legs. Lean your torso forward, leading with your right hand. When you can't go any farther, bend your body so your right hand touches your leg or the ground. Your left arm and your chin should be pointing straight up. Take a few breaths in this position. Repeat on the other side.

Why this pose is good for you: This twisting pose opens your hips and shoulders, strengthens your back muscles, and can improve your balance with practice.

Wide-Legged Forward Bend

Sanskrit name: Prasarita Padottanasana

Stand with your feet wide apart and your toes facing forward. Breathe in and raise your arms up. Then, with a straight back, breathe out and fold your body slowly forward, letting your arms lower with your body. Touch the floor or grab your elbows and hang your torso over your toes for five deep breaths.

Why this pose is good for you: Wide-Legged Forward Bend stretches the backs of your legs and can relieve tension in your neck.

Child's Pose

Sanskrit name: Balasana

Sit up with your knees underneath you. Fold your body forward, slowly sliding your arms directly in front of you until your forehead touches the ground. Take deep breaths as you rest in this position.

Why this pose is good for you: This pose allows your neck and spine to relax while stretching your lower back, hips, and thighs.

Mindfulness Tip: As you're breathing, notice the sensation of your breath as it is moving into your body and out. See if you can stay with the sensation of your breath from the very beginning of each breath to the end of each breath.

Cow and Cat Poses

Sanskrit names: Bitilasana and Marjaryasana

Start on your hands and knees with wrists directly underneath your shoulders and knees underneath your hips. As you inhale, slowly arch your back and turn your gaze forward for Cow Pose. As you exhale, slowly round your back and turn your gaze downward for Cat Pose. Repeat a few times.

Why these poses are good for you: Flowing between these two positions opens your chest, strengthens your abs, and stretches your spine and neck.

Sanskrit name: Adho Mukha Svanasana

Get into a plank position with your hands directly underneath your shoulders and your feet hip-width apart. Breathe out as you slowly press your hips toward the ceiling to form an inverted V. Keep equal pressure on your hands and feet.

Why this pose is good for you: Downward-Facing Dog deeply stretches your back muscles and your calves. It's also a good strengthening exercise for your arms.

Downward-Facing Dog

Mindfulness Tip: As you're breathing, notice the sensations in the backs of your legs. Is there a tightness there? A stretching? Maybe discomfort?

Legs Up The Wall Pose

Sanskrit name: Viparita Karani

Place your yoga mat perpendicular to a wall. Sit facing the wall with your legs straight in front of you. Place a yoga bolster or small pillow several inches away from the wall. Scoot toward the wall, slowly bringing your legs up onto the wall, until your lower back rests on the pillow. Lean your head and back onto the ground. Keep legs straight and locked together and your arms out to your sides in a goal post position, with palms facing up. Take five to ten deep breaths in this position.

Why this pose is good for you: This inversion pose can relieve tension in your back and soothe tired legs and feet.

Cobra Pose

Sanskrit name: Bhujangasana

Lie facedown on the yoga mat. Place the tops of your feet flat on the floor. Bend your arms, keeping your elbows close to your body and your hands palms-down at your sides as if you were about to do a push-up. Spread your fingers wide, then slowly arch your back as you lift your torso upward. Your head can face forward or you can tilt your chin up toward the ceiling. Hold the stretch for five breaths.

Why this pose is good for you: Cobra Pose is a great stretch for your spine and can help reduce lower back pain.

Corpse Pose

Sanskrit name: Savasana

Lie on your back with your legs straight in front of you and your arms at your sides. Face your palms up and let your knees drop open comfortably. Take deep breaths as you rest in this position.

Why this pose is good for you:
Corpse Pose is used at the end of a yoga routine as a relaxing but rejuvenating finish.

"IT DOES NOT MATTER HOW SLOWLY YOU GO AS LONG AS YOU DO NOT STOP." – CONFUCIUS

Just Breathe

When you focus on your breathing, you will simply watch and feel your breath. Deep breathing sends signals to the body to calm down. It can make the mind clearer, and it delivers more oxygen to the lungs and heart.

Sit cross-legged or lie on a yoga mat — whatever is most comfortable! The following breathing exercises are organized by difficulty, from easier to more challenging.

ABDOMINAL BREATHING

When to do it: Before a stressful event or when you're feeling nervous
How to do it: Place one hand on your chest and the other on your belly. Inhale deeply, then exhale deeply. Notice the slight change in sensations as your chest rises and then falls. Repeat as many times as you'd like.
What it does: This breathing method helps you find focus and peace.

EQUAL BREATHING

When to do it: When you're trying to meditate
How to do it: Inhale deeply for four seconds, then exhale deeply for four seconds. Repeat as many times as you'd like.
What it does: This is a relaxing exercise.

ALTERNATE NOSTRIL BREATHING

When to do it: When you need to focus
How to do it: Cover your left nostril and breathe in, then move your finger to cover your right nostril and breathe out. Now breathe in through your left nostril, then move your finger to cover your left nostril and breathe out. Repeat as many times as you'd like.
What it does: This exercise is energizing.

RELAXING BREATH

When to do it: When you need to fall asleep
How to do it: Inhale for four seconds, then exhale for eight seconds. Repeat five times.
What it does: This exercise is a natural tranquilizer.

STIMULATING BREATH

When to do it: When you need a confidence boost
How to do it: Inhale and exhale rapidly through your nose while keeping your mouth lightly closed. Do this for no more than ten seconds.
What it does: This invigorating exercise gives you an energy boost and focus.

"I'D RATHER REGRET THE THINGS I'VE DONE THAN REGRET THE THINGS I HAVEN'T DONE." – LUCILLE BALL

Take a Staycation

A short break can do a lot for your peace of mind. Just like you recharge your phone, sometimes you need to recharge your mind and body. Your "staycation" can be done alone or with others — whichever seems more relaxing to you. Look at the itineraries here to get you started, but feel free to tailor them however you'd like.

ITINERARY 1: CREATIVE SESSION

If you had to pick a favorite place where you live, what would it be? It could be an inspiring place like a beautiful park or a lookout point. Or it could be a library, a café, or even your own front yard. Once you've settled on a special spot, bring sketching, writing, or painting supplies to this place. Make sure you have a comfortable spot to sit, then observe your surroundings. Notice the details, from the smells and sounds to the emotions you experience, as you sit.

Now try to re-create this space in the creative medium of your choice — a story, poem, drawing, song, comic book, short movie — whatever you want. Express yourself via your chosen art medium. It doesn't have to be perfect. When you're done, challenge yourself to share your work with at least one person.

ITINERARY 2: CALMING GETAWAY

Take some time to research nearby arboretums, observatories, nature reserves, and trails. You may be surprised at the beauty that's hiding in your own town. Choose the place that looks most serene to you. Someplace with a view of a lake, ocean, mountain, meadow, or river is a good option!

Plan for a long bike ride, hike, or walk on a sunny morning. Take a small blanket, a book, sunscreen, some snacks, and water in a backpack. When you find the perfect spot, stop and read for an hour or two. Or, if you feel inspired, write or draw in a notebook.

For tips on starting your own nature journal, turn to page 118.

ITINERARY 3: EDUCATIONAL EXCURSION

Start your day at a museum or zoo that's inspiring to you. If there is a temporary exhibit, workshop, or presentation that especially piques your interest, take advantage of it! Be sure to schedule a few hours to explore, so you don't feel rushed. Go alone or with a friend who is willing to stroll with you at a leisurely pace.

As you walk through the exhibits, take the time to read everything and learn something new. Bring along a journal so you can take notes or sketch the most inspiring things you see or learn. Don't be afraid to find a seat in your favorite exhibit and stay awhile. Afterward, head to the library where you can check out a book on something that you'd love to learn more about.

ITINERARY 4: DOUBLE FEATURE

Take a trip to the library and browse the movie section, or browse through Netflix or YouTube. There's a documentary on just about everything, right? Pick a documentary about a subject that's always interested you, such as a certain event in history, a specific place in the world, or a person or career choice you admire. Now pick a documentary on a subject you know nothing about and weren't really interested in before. It should be something you would never normally watch. Head home, pop some popcorn, and get ready for a double feature. Start with the movie you never imagined watching.

You may be surprised what you learn.

ITINERARY 5: WINDOW SHOPPING

Visit your favorite mall or shopping area with one goal: don't spend any money! Instead, have fun browsing. This is a fun activity to do with friends or family. Get inspired by what you see — a great outfit idea, a bedroom decorating tip, a cool poster, or even an interesting person you encounter.

Feel free to touch, try on, or take pictures of your favorite things. But no buying! If you want to make a game of it, create a scavenger hunt or a photo challenge and set a time limit. Or you can window shop for fantastical things such as furnishings for your dream home, a gown for a royal ball, or what you might need for a trip around the world.

ITINERARY 6: VIRTUAL VACATION

What's one place you'd love to visit in the world? The Taj Mahal? The Great Wall of China? The Eiffel Tower? Machu Picchu? The Grand Canyon? Angkor Wat? Head to the library and check out a bunch of books on that location. Travel books are an obvious choice, but don't forget about historical biographies and novels that can provide backstory on your dream destination. A librarian can help you gather the best materials.

If you're interested in traveling abroad to a non-English-speaking country, you could check out a language book or CD or download a free language-learning app such as Duolingo. Look in the cookbook section to explore the local cuisine. Then browse the CDs to find some local music. There may even be a DVD for a travel show episode that features your location of choice. If you're really inspired, you could throw a mini party that re-creates your dream destination!

"NOT ALL WHO WANDER ARE LOST." – J.R.R. TOLKIEN

Head Outdoors

Feeling connected to nature is good for you. It can help you feel healthier and happier by bettering your mood, reducing anxiety, and improving brain function. Imagine what a few hours outdoors can do for your soul. When it comes to beating stress, this is as natural as it gets!

Sunlight and fresh air are natural mood lifters. Being outside can help you feel more energized, less stressed, and can increase happiness.

Mindfulness Tip: When you're outside, take time to notice things that really call to you. Maybe it's the color of a flower, the smell of freshly cut grass, or even an ant crawling on the sidewalk. Savor those things that you're drawn to!

Go outside! Try:

- GOING ON A LONG BIKE RIDE AROUND A NATURE RESERVE OR A LAKE.
- RENTING A KAYAK OR CANOE WITH A FRIEND.
- TAKING A TRIP TO A SKI HILL WHERE YOU CAN PRACTICE YOUR SNOWBOARDING SKILLS.
- GOING ON A HIKE THAT LEADS TO A WATERFALL OR A LOOKOUT POINT.
- VISITING A BOTANICAL GARDEN OR ARBORETUM.
- CAMPING OUT WITH YOUR FAMILY.
- GOING FOR A WALK IN A NEARBY PARK AND TAKING PHOTOS OF TREES OR BIRDS.
- STARTING A NATURE JOURNAL (SEE PAGE 118).
- SPENDING AN AFTERNOON AT A PETTING ZOO OR FARM.
- GOING APPLE PICKING WITH FRIENDS.
- TAKING A WALK WITH YOUR FAMILY AROUND YOUR NEIGHBORHOOD AFTER DINNER.
- MAKING A SNOWMAN WITH YOUR SIBLINGS OR SOME FRIENDS.
- OFFERING TO MOW THE LAWN OR RAKE LEAVES FOR YOUR PARENTS OR A NEIGHBOR.
- PLANTING FLOWERS IN A GARDEN OR IN A POT. IF YOU DON'T HAVE ROOM FOR A GARDEN AT YOUR HOME, YOU CAN ALWAYS VOLUNTEER FOR YOUR CITY'S PARKS AND RECREATION DEPARTMENT.
- READING A BOOK ON THE BEACH OR ON A PARK BENCH.

Even if you can't get outdoors right away, there are other things you can do to help you feel more connected to nature. Here are a few ideas:

- CHANGE THE BACKGROUND ON YOUR COMPUTER OR PHONE TO YOUR FAVORITE NATURE PHOTO. SIMPLY LOOKING AT PICTURES OF NATURE CAN HELP YOU DE-STRESS.
- WATCH A DOCUMENTARY ABOUT A NATIONAL PARK YOU'D LIKE TO VISIT.
- CREATE A PINTEREST BOARD OF YOUR FAVORITE NATURE PHOTOS.
- SET UP A WORKSPACE NEAR A WINDOW. NOW YOU CAN DO HOMEWORK WITH A VIEW!
- DECORATE YOUR ROOM WITH PICTURES OF YOUR FAVORITE OUTDOOR SCENES.

"EVERYTHING HAS BEAUTY, BUT NOT EVERYONE SEES IT." – CONFUCIUS

Get Some Sun

Getting outside can give you a quick burst of happiness for another reason — sunshine! Just 15 minutes a day can make a difference.

Over the last couple of decades, the sun has gotten a bad rap due to the prevalence of skin cancer. But the truth is that we need a little bit of sun every day — with the protection of sunscreen, of course. There are many reasons why sunshine is good for you. Here are a few:

- SUNLIGHT HELPS YOUR BODY PRODUCE VITAMIN D, WHICH KEEPS YOUR BONES HEALTHY AND STRONG.

- SUN HELPS REGULATE YOUR BIOLOGICAL CLOCK. SUNSHINE SIGNALS TO YOUR BODY THAT IT'S DAYTIME, AND DARKNESS SIGNALS THAT IT'S NIGHTTIME.

- SOME PEOPLE GET THE WINTER BLUES, BUT SUNSHINE CAN HELP FIGHT OFF SEASONAL DEPRESSION. IN SHORT, SUNLIGHT MAKES YOU HAPPY!

You don't have to drastically change your routine to incorporate more sunshine into your day. Here are some easy habits you can start that will give your body the vitamin D it needs. Even if you live in an area that gets cold during the winter, you can still do many of these activities year-round. You'll just have to layer appropriately. Don't forget a hat!

INSTEAD OF READING INSIDE . . . MOVE OUTDOORS TO A PARK BENCH.

INSTEAD OF TAKING THE BUS TO SCHOOL . . . RIDE YOUR BIKE.

INSTEAD OF DOING HOMEWORK AT YOUR DESK . . . DO IT OUTSIDE.

INSTEAD OF LISTENING TO MUSIC IN YOUR ROOM . . . LISTEN TO IT WHILE YOU GO FOR A WALK.

INSTEAD OF TAKING A NAP ON THE COUCH . . . NAP ON A BLANKET IN THE GRASS.

INSTEAD OF RUNNING ON A TREADMILL . . . GO FOR A RUN THROUGH YOUR NEIGHBORHOOD.

INSTEAD OF WATCHING TV . . . WATCH A SUNSET.

INSTEAD OF EATING LUNCH INSIDE . . . FIND A PICNIC TABLE UNDER THE SUN.

INSTEAD OF LETTING YOUR DOG OUT IN THE BACKYARD . . . TAKE HIM FOR A WALK.

"A JOURNEY OF A THOUSAND MILES BEGINS WITH A SINGLE STEP." – LAO TZU

Visualize

Visualization is the practice of creating a mental image. The technique is often used to help professionals such as athletes, actors, doctors, and lawyers prepare for big events. You can use visualization as a rehearsal for a challenge you're about to take on, or you can use it as an escape when you're feeling stressed. It can give you more confidence or give you a sense of calm — either way, it's good for you!

When you practice visualization, it's important to consider all five senses. What are you smelling? Hearing? Feeling? Seeing? Tasting? Try visualizing for five minutes each night before bed.

Before you start visualizing, find a quiet place to sit or lie down, then close your eyes.

IF YOU'RE THINKING, "I NEED TO STEP AWAY FOR A MINUTE."

Think of this visualization as a break that will help you relax when you're feeling particularly overwhelmed.

Brush any stressful or concerning images to the side and make room for some good thoughts.

Close your eyes. Imagine your body is so light that it floats off the ground and soars gracefully into the sky. Picture what your home or school looks like from above. Now imagine yourself soaring through the clouds. Look below. What do you see? Now look above and admire the never-ending sky. When you're ready, gently float back down to Earth. Land softly in the grass in your front yard or in your favorite park. Take a few more deep breaths. When you're ready, open your eyes.

IF YOU'RE THINKING, "I NEED TO GET OUT OF HERE."

When you're feeling stressed out, a mental vacation is almost as good as a real one.

Imagine a secluded beach or another serene place, such as a cabin in a quiet forest; a kayak on a smooth, clear lake; or a bench in a sunny park. Now imagine you're in that perfect place, seeing it through your own eyes. Think about your other senses and the ways the environment is calming each one.

Visualization exercises can also help you fall asleep.

IF YOU'RE THINKING, "I CAN DO THIS . . . BUT I'M NERVOUS."

This visualization can bring you courage when you need it most.

Find a comfortable position on the ground with your legs crossed or kneeling, then close your eyes and straighten your back and shoulders. Breathe deeply in and out. When your breath is steady, begin to imagine a majestic mountain in front of you. Admire it from afar. Visualize the trees, sky, and water surrounding it. Then "zoom in" your focus to the mountain. Get closer, and closer. Now imagine you are the mountain — its peak is your head and its base is your legs. No matter what the season, the mountain sits unchanged and strong. Visualize the mountain standing strong through changes in foliage, snowfall, rainstorms, intense heat, and dense fog. No matter what comes your way, you can sit unchanged and strong, like the mountain. When you're ready, open your eyes.

IF YOU'RE THINKING, "I COULD NEVER DO THAT."

Through your own eyes, imagine yourself doing the action you believe you cannot do. Visualize every single step of the way. For instance, if you want to learn how to play a song on the guitar, imagine yourself opening your guitar case, picking up the guitar, touching each string, reading the music notes, strumming each chord, and hearing the song come together. You could even imagine yourself messing up a note, then recovering quickly. Sometimes it can be helpful to realize that making a mistake doesn't mean failure.

IF YOU'RE THINKING, "I CAN'T BELIEVE THAT HAPPENED."

It's usually not helpful to dwell on the past, but if something is bothering you and you just can't shake it, visualization can help. Imagine the moment as a movie, but change anything about the scene for the better. Fix your mistakes, change what you said, or alter what someone else did. Replay the revised version in your head a few times. Then move on.

IF YOU'RE THINKING, "I CAN'T SHAKE THIS BAD FEELING."

When you're feeling tense, this visualization may help melt away your fears.

Sit on the floor or lie down and close your eyes. Imagine that you've stepped out of your body and are looking at yourself while you meditate. Observe yourself from afar. Walk a full circle around your body. Now pick up a paintbrush and dip it onto a palette. Starting with your favorite color, brush each part of your body slowly from your head to your toes. Take time to re-dip your paintbrush and choose a different color for each body part. Imagine the stress melting away with each brush stroke and your muscles transforming from tensed to relaxed as the paint touches your skin. Once you've painted your entire body, take a few more deep breaths. When you're ready, open your eyes.

Some studies have found that consistent visualizing can help you reach your potential when combined with practicing. For example, if you're trying to master a particular dance move, imagine yourself executing the move for a few minutes before you physically practice. Don't rush — the visualization should take about the same amount of time as the act would in real life.

"COURAGE IS RESISTANCE TO FEAR, MASTERY OF FEAR — NOT ABSENCE OF FEAR." – MARK TWAIN

Give Yourself a Massage

Massage therapy is a great way to relax and relieve stress. With the following self-massage strategies, you won't have to go to a spa for an ahh moment. Before you start a massage, gently rub your favorite lotion into your hands. Then sit or lie comfortably in a quiet space.

Mindfulness Tip: As you go through each of these massages, make sure you notice the feeling of tension gently loosening and the area around each part "letting go" a bit. Keep your attention with the sensation.

EYE MASSAGE

Perfect for: soothing tired eyes after a long night of studying or staring at a computer screen.

What you do: Since you'll be massaging around your eyes, don't use lotion on your hands for this massage. With your eyes closed, place your thumbs at the inner corner of each eye socket. Using a small circular movement, softly massage the area. Move slowly toward the end of your eyebrows and back around the bottom of your eye socket until you reach your nose. Repeat several times.

JAW MASSAGE

Perfect for: releasing tension if you clenched your jaw while you slept or during a stressful test.

What you do: Clench your teeth to flex your jaw muscles. Place two fingers directly on each muscle, just below your ears. Now open your mouth slightly while moving your fingers in a circular motion. Repeat for about 30 seconds.

FULL FACE MASSAGE

Perfect for: removing stress from your face at the end of a long day.

What you do: Make fists with your hands. Using your knuckles, trace your jaw from your ears to your chin. Repeat 15 times. Now, with your thumbs pointing down, run your knuckles from the bridge of your nose to the outer corners of your eyes. When you end, your thumbs will be pointing up. Repeat 15 times. Finally, with the thumbs of your fists pointing up, run your knuckles from the center of your forehead to the ends of your eyebrows. Repeat 15 times.

SCALP MASSAGE

Perfect for: releasing tension before bed.

What you do: Don't use lotion on your hands, since they'll be in contact with your hair. Using your fingers, begin massaging in a circular motion from the back of your head to the front, focusing on the hairline. When you reach your temples, massage in small circular motions, moving toward the center of your head. Continue from the top of the head to the back of the head. Now place your thumbs at the base of your neck and your hands near the top of your head. Massage the base of your neck by moving your thumbs in a circular motion.

HAND MASSAGE

Perfect for: relieving strain from sore fingers after a long day of typing, drawing, writing, or playing an instrument.

What you do: Flex your left hand open and closed a few times. Now take the thumb and pointer finger of your right hand and rub each finger from base to tip. Pull and twist the finger a little as you do. Repeat on the right hand.

FOOT MASSAGE

Perfect for: re-energizing tired feet after a long day of walking, sports practice, or a competition.

What you do: Rest your left foot on your right knee. Holding the left heel with your right hand, use your left hand to squeeze and tug each toe. Now massage and twist each toe. Finally, use the thumbs of both hands to make a strong circular movement on the arch and sole of your foot. Repeat with the right foot.

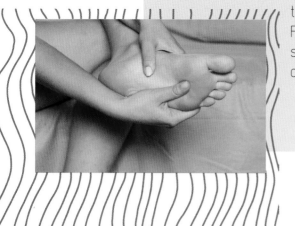

If any of these massages cause pain, stop! Always listen to your body.

NECK MASSAGE

Perfect for: if you slept in an uncomfortable position and wake up feeling sore.

What you do: Place your hands just below the back of your neck and apply pressure with your fingertips. As you slowly pull forward, bend your neck forward for a ten-second stretch. Now wrap your hands lightly around your neck so your fingertips touch the back of your neck, with one hand on each side of your spine. Slide your fingers from the sides of your neck to the tops of your shoulders. Repeat three times. Now slide your fingers up and down the back of your neck. Repeat three times.

SHOULDER MASSAGE

Perfect for: relieving tense shoulder muscles.

What you do: Place your left hand on your right shoulder and squeeze. Slowly rotate the right shoulder backward a few times, then rub your hand up and down your upper arm a few times. Repeat on the other side. Place your left elbow in the right hand, then lightly knock between the neck and right shoulder. Repeat on the other side. Using your fingertips, apply pressure to the center of your chest (just under your collar bone) and continue applying pressure as you move your fingers toward your shoulders. Repeat a few times. Finish by making a few circular motions in the same area.

During a massage, you should never apply pressure directly to the spine or the throat.

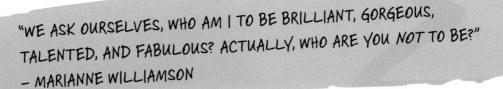

"WE ASK OURSELVES, WHO AM I TO BE BRILLIANT, GORGEOUS, TALENTED, AND FABULOUS? ACTUALLY, WHO ARE YOU *NOT* TO BE?"
– MARIANNE WILLIAMSON

Have a Cup of Tea

Teas have great health benefits. Here are just a few that can help calm your mind and soothe your body.

If you don't like the taste of tea, add a spoonful of honey and a drop of lemon juice or milk.

Mindfulness Tip: As you are making and drinking your tea, remember to enjoy the smell of the tea as it brews, the warmth of your tea cup in your hand, and the gentle curling of the steam as it leaves your cup. Being mindful of these details can help you find peace.

CHAMOMILE

Some health experts say chamomile helps calm your nerves and helps you fall asleep. Drink a cup an hour before you go to bed.

CINNAMON

The antioxidants in cinnamon could help keep you healthy, and even just *smelling* cinnamon may give you a mental boost!

GREEN

Green tea has an ingredient called theanine that may calm your anxieties and help you relax. But this tea contains caffeine, so don't drink it before bed!

PASSIONFLOWER

Passionflower may help soothe your mind by calming mental activity. That means it could reduce nervousness and may help you fall asleep.

PEPPERMINT

If you have an upset stomach, peppermint can calm the feeling. It can also give you an energy boost that may help keep you focused and confident.

GINGER

Ginger is known for its soothing properties. It can help reduce stress-induced indigestion and alleviate sore, tense muscles.

YERBA MATE

Health experts say this kind of tea offers a balanced energy boost thanks to the caffeine within it. It is said to help overcome both mental and physical fatigue.

LAVENDER

Lavender tea has a calming aroma, and it may help soothe your nerves too. Drink a cup an hour before bed or before a stressful event to help you relax.

"TO LOVE ONESELF IS THE BEGINNING OF A LIFELONG ROMANCE." – OSCAR WILDE

Exude Confidence

Even when your mouth is closed, your body is speaking through your facial expressions, shoulders, eyes, leg placement, hand gestures, and more. First impressions are often made based on body language. If your shoulders are slumped, your arms crossed, and your eyes cast downward, you may not look very approachable. But if you send out more positive signals to the world, you may be more likely to receive them. Positivity attracts positivity, and good body language makes you look friendly, confident, and trustworthy.

For good posture tips, turn to page 122.

1. KEEP YOUR HEAD UP.

If you catch someone's gaze, it will make it easier to say hi, share a smile, or ask a question. If you're looking down, you can't do that! Make eye contact when you talk — and when you listen. It shows that you are enjoying the conversation.

2. RELAX YOUR SHOULDERS AND ARMS.

When you're tense, your shoulders shrug up to your ears. And when your arms are crossed, it can give people the impression that you are distant or defensive. Take a deep breath, then relax your shoulders and arms as you breathe out. Wiggle them a little bit to loosen up. Let your arms fall naturally at your sides.

3. MOVE SLOWLY.

Try not to fidget, tap your feet, touch your face, or flail your hands. You'll look nervous! It's OK to use hand gestures when you talk, but try not to overdo it. Move confidently, calmly, and deliberately.

4. SMILE AND NOD.

To show you're listening and interested in a conversation, smile and nod — or laugh when it's appropriate. A smile gives a vote of confidence to someone else. It may make them feel more comfortable around you.

Create a Time Budget

You're at the mall with friends and you have $40. You buy a shirt for $30 and lunch for $10. Now your friends want to get ice cream, but you can't because you've already spent your budget.

Imagine if you treated time the same way you treat money. There are 24 hours in each day. So how will you best spend each one? Creating a time budget can help you manage stress, be more productive, and make sure there's still time for fun.

24-HOUR BUDGET

TAKE OUT A PIECE OF BLANK PAPER. DRAW FOUR COLUMNS ON YOUR PAGE, TITLED "SPEND," "SAVE," "INVEST," AND "GIVE." FOLLOW THE STEPS BELOW TO COME UP WITH A 24-HOUR TIME BUDGET TAILORED JUST FOR YOU.

1. SPEND

Write down the amount of hours you spend in a day on "non-negotiable" commitments such as school, sleep, and getting ready each morning. Tally up the total.

2. SAVE

List some of your favorite ways to spend "me time" and how long each idea takes. For example, reading a novel for one hour, going for a 30-minute run, or winding down before bed (see page 140).

3. INVEST

Tally up how long you need each day to reach your goals and accomplish tasks. Taking a drawing class for one hour or spending two hours on homework are great examples.

4. GIVE

Consider how much time you'd like to spend each day on others: whether it's volunteering, spending quality time with your family, or hanging out with your friends.

5. COMPLETE YOUR SCHEDULE

Now comes the challenging part: trying to fit all your ideas into 24 hours! On a new sheet of paper, create an hour-by-hour schedule for one day. Once you've completed it, you'll become more aware of how you are spending your time. When you have a good idea of how you're spending 24 hours, you can move up to creating a weeklong time budget.

Squash Your Stress

Stress balls — or more appropriately anti-stress balls — can help relieve tension one squeeze at a time. Repeated tensing and relaxing of the muscles is a great relaxation strategy. The stress ball helps relieve tense hand and arm muscles and releases energy each time you squeeze. It's also a great way to divert your attention quickly.

YOU WILL NEED:

2 balloons of the same color (not blown up)
4-oz container of modeling dough
a permanent marker
scissors

Anti-Stress Ball Craft

Directions:

Cut off the rolled tip at the end of both balloons. Stuff one balloon with modeling dough (it works best if you stretch the neck of the balloon with two fingers and push a large ball of dough into the balloon) until the balloon is full. Depending on the size of your balloon, you may not use all of the modeling dough.

Squeeze, roll, and flatten the balloon, holding the open end lightly to make sure no modeling dough escapes, until all air bubbles have been removed. Knot the balloon tightly and trim the excess. Now slide the second balloon over the first to cover the knotted end. Trim the excess. Decorate with permanent markers – a happy face is always a good choice!

Now you can squeeze and squish this ball in your hands whenever you feel anxious, nervous, or scared.

"GREAT MINDS DISCUSS IDEAS; AVERAGE MINDS DISCUSS EVENTS; SMALL MINDS DISCUSS PEOPLE."
– ELEANOR ROOSEVELT

Tech Detox

There are many reasons why you should step away from technology every now and then. Not only can bright screens disrupt sleep patterns, but social media can also make you feel bad about yourself. When you see a perfectly edited version of someone else's life, it can make you feel as though your life is lacking.

WITH SMARTPHONES, SOCIAL MEDIA IS ALWAYS CLOSE BY. IF YOU HAVE A BIG PAPER DUE, OR A PARTICULAR SOCIAL MEDIA PLATFORM IS CAUSING YOU STRESS FOR ANY REASON, TRY DELETING YOUR MOST-FREQUENTED SOCIAL MEDIA APP(S) OFF YOUR PHONE FOR A FEW DAYS. IF YOU DON'T MISS IT, DELETING YOUR ACCOUNT IS ALWAYS AN OPTION.

Here are just a few ways to take a tech detox.

ONE-HOUR BREAK

For just one hour, turn off all of your electronic devices, including the TV, and put your phone in a drawer. What will you do with a screen-free, unconnected hour? That's up to you. It might be difficult at first, but rising to the challenge can be so satisfying.

NO TECHNOLOGY AFTER 8 P.M.

Starting tonight, make a rule for yourself: "no tech after 8 p.m." Find something else to do! Read a magazine, draw a picture, clean your room, play a board game with a sibling or parent, or write a letter to a friend.

TECH-FREE SATURDAY

Feeling a little more freedom? Now that your phone isn't quite so handcuffed to your body, you may be able to take the next step: a whole day without technology. No phone, no Internet, no computer. When you tune back in tomorrow, you'll be surprised to learn that you didn't miss much. Nothing is as urgent as it often seems.

A WEEK OFF

Warning: this is advanced! A weeklong detox is most easily accomplished during a time when school is not in session, such as winter break, spring break, or summer break. If you'd like, you can even give your friends a heads-up — or challenge them to participate! See how many days in a row you can last with no phone, no Internet, and no computer. If you break down, don't completely give up. Start fresh the next day.

"TO LIVE IS THE RAREST THING IN THE WORLD. MOST PEOPLE EXIST, THAT IS ALL." – OSCAR WILDE

Clean Your Room

Organization can give you a sense of control, and it can help you overcome feelings of being overwhelmed. A clean bedroom can instantly make you feel less stressed. Here's how you can get there.

TO GET ORGANIZED, YOU HAVE TO GET A LITTLE *DISORGANIZED* FIRST. MAKE SURE YOU HAVE ENOUGH TIME TO COMPLETE THIS PROJECT BEFORE YOU START. IF YOU PAUSE IN THE MIDDLE, YOU COULD GET MORE STRESSED!

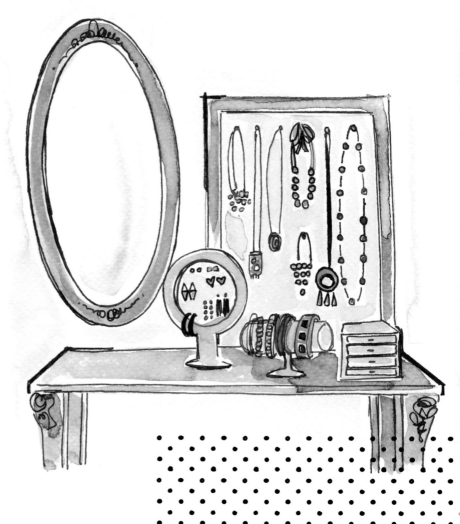

How to do it:

1. Tackle one space at a time. It might be a drawer, a dresser, or a bookshelf. Remove all items from the space and place them on the floor or a table so you can see everything clearly. Things might get messier before they get clean – and that's OK! You'll also need to clear a space nearby temporarily so you can more easily accomplish step two.

2. Create three piles: throw it away, give it away, or keep it. Now sort your belongings into the piles. Make quick decisions and don't second-guess yourself! If you have problems making decisions, create a "maybe" pile to revisit at the end.

3. When you've finished sorting, put the throw away and give away piles to the side, and start arranging the items you'll keep. Everything should have a specific place that makes sense and is easily accessible. Create a dedicated "staging area" (like a chair or side table) where you can keep your books, bag, keys, as well as tomorrow's outfit. A dedicated "command center" (like a desk or shelf) is a great place to store homework, a planner and calendar, upcoming projects, and school supplies. In other words, your mittens shouldn't be in a desk drawer, and your calculator shouldn't be in your closet!

Here are some more organization tips:

ARRANGE BOOKS BY SIZE, COLOR, OR SUBJECT.

ORGANIZE CLOTHING BY COLOR, SEASON, STYLE, OR OCCASION.

JEWELRY AND ACCESSORIES CAN BE STACKED, HUNG, OR STORED.

ADD LABELS TO FOLDERS, BOXES, OR JARS TO MAKE EVERYTHING EASIER TO FIND.

Set aside ten minutes to de-clutter every night. It's amazing how much more organized you can feel in just a few minutes!

"THERE ARE NO SHORTCUTS TO ANY PLACE WORTH GOING." – BEVERLY SILLS

Simplify Your Wardrobe

One way to de-stress your life is to simplify your wardrobe. Look at all the stuff in your closet or dresser. Do you use all of it? Do you love all of it? Do you need all of it? Do you even want all of it?

The goal of this exercise is to get rid of anything that doesn't fit well, that doesn't make you feel beautiful and confident, and that doesn't feel like "you." If you spend one afternoon purging, there's a good chance you'll end up with a giant bag of donations. Once you've cleared out the clutter, you'll feel lighter and happier. It will be much easier to choose an outfit when you love all of your clothes! Plus, you'll feel great in anything you put on.

DONATE UNWANTED CLOTHING TO AN ORGANIZATION LIKE GOODWILL, SALVATION ARMY, OR ST. VINCENT DE PAUL. FORMAL WEAR AND DRESSES CAN BE DONATED TO A PLACE CALLED HOME'S CINDERELLA & PRINCE CHARMING PROJECT.

Create a Capsule Wardrobe

A capsule wardrobe is a minimalist, tightly edited wardrobe that can easily be mixed and matched to create many looks. Did you know that with just 12 items you can create over a hundred outfits? It's true. 4 shirts + 3 bottoms + 4 jackets or sweaters + 1 dress + 3 pairs of shoes = 100 different outfit combinations!

You might not be able to edit your wardrobe down that much, especially if you live in a place that gets really cold in the winter and really hot in the summer. But finding 12 perfect pieces is a great goal for each season's weekly wardrobe.

Many capsule wardrobes are made up of simple styles and basic colors that never go out of fashion, such as a black v-neck T-shirt, a great fitting pair of jeans, and a comfortable pair of sandals. Here are some steps to get you started:

REMOVE ALL OF YOUR CLOTHING FROM YOUR CLOSET AND YOUR DRAWERS.

GET RID OF ANYTHING YOU HAVEN'T WORN IN THE PAST YEAR AND ANYTHING THAT'S STAINED OR TORN.

NOW PURGE ANYTHING THAT'S OUT OF STYLE OR THAT DOESN'T MATCH ANYTHING ELSE YOU OWN.

TRY ON THE REST. GET RID OF ANYTHING THAT DOESN'T FIT WELL OR THAT DOESN'T MAKE YOU FEEL GREAT.

ASSESS WHAT IS LEFT. IF YOU NEED TO EDIT MORE, KEEP CLOTHES THAT ARE IN THE SAME COLOR FAMILY, THAT ARE ESPECIALLY COMFORTABLE, AND THAT CAN BE EASILY MIXED AND MATCHED.

"YOU CAN'T START THE NEXT CHAPTER IF YOU KEEP READING THE LAST." – UNKNOWN

Stretch

Stretching can provide an instant release of built-up tension.
Try one of these stretches for a quick but invigorating exercise.

For full-body stretches,
check out Strike a (Yoga)
Pose on page 12.

JAW STRETCH

Hold a thumb to your chin and apply pressure to create a slight resistance. Open and close your jaw 10 times.

NECK ROLL

Tilt your chin to your chest. Roll your left ear to your left shoulder. Roll back to the center. Roll your right ear to your right shoulder. Return to center. Repeat 10 times.

NECK STRETCH

Tilt your left ear to your left shoulder as your right arm relaxes at your side. Reach your left hand over your head and let your fingers rest on your right temple. Apply a little bit of pressure as you stretch. Repeat on the right side.

SHOULDER ROTATION

Stand with your back against a wall. Bend your arms at the elbow to make 90-degree angles, and hold your elbows against the wall. Slowly rotate your left arm downward (so your palm touches the wall) and your right arm upward (so the back of your hand touches the wall), then alternate. Repeat 10 times.

SHOULDER STRETCH

This stretch begins on the ground with your knees directly under your hips and your wrists directly underneath your shoulders. Lift your left arm and slide it through the space between your right arm and leg. It should be touching the floor. Rotate your upper body until you feel the stretch. Hold for 10 seconds. Repeat on the other side.

CHEST STRETCH

Lie on your right side with your legs bent at a 90-degree angle. Reach your arms out in front of you so they are perpendicular to your body. Reach your left arm up and over, creating an arch movement, until the arm reaches the ground on the opposite side. Let your gaze follow. Stretch for about 10 seconds. Repeat on the other side.

ARM CIRCLES

With a straight arm extended directly in front of you, make five slow circles backward. Make five slow circles forward. Repeat on the other side.

If any of these stretches cause pain, stop! Always listen to your body.

"A PERSON WHO NEVER MADE A MISTAKE NEVER TRIED ANYTHING NEW." – ALBERT EINSTEIN

Progressive Muscle Relaxation

In this exercise, you'll tense and release as many muscles in your body as you can, starting with your toes and working up to your head.

Be sure to keep breathing steadily throughout these exercises!

DURATION: 5-10 minutes

WHEN: morning or night

YOU WILL NEED:

a yoga mat, bed, or couch

a quiet space

Directions:

Lie on your back with your arms at your sides and your palms facing up.

Tense your left foot by pointing or flexing it for five seconds, then let the muscles relax for ten seconds. Repeat with your calf, hamstring, and glutes. Repeat on the right side.

Tense your abdominal muscles for five seconds, then release.

Clench your left hand into a fist for five seconds, then let the muscles relax for ten seconds. Now tense your biceps, and then your shoulder. Repeat on the right side.

Finish by tensing each part of your face for five seconds, then relaxing for ten seconds in this order: clench your jaw, smile big, scrunch your nose, squeeze your eyes closed, raise your eyebrows.

SEVERAL STUDIES SHOW THAT THIS EXERCISE CAN REDUCE PULSE RATES, BLOOD PRESSURE, AND RESPIRATION RATES, RESULTING IN LESS STRESS!

Mindfulness Tip: When each muscle is tensed, notice how you're feeling throughout your body. Then with the release of each muscle, notice how the feelings throughout your whole body change.

"THE ONLY PERSON YOU ARE DESTINED TO BECOME IS THE PERSON YOU DECIDE TO BE." – RALPH WALDO EMERSON

Take a Bath

Baths can be both relaxing and healing. They can soothe muscles, calm some skin inflammations, and help you fall asleep. Taking a bath can even help you feel better when you're sick. If you're going to take a soak, you might as well make it extra special. Try one of these bath-boosting ingredients for an easy pick-me-up or calm-me-down.

Mindfulness Tip: As you immerse your body in the water, notice how the water feels against your skin. Is it warm? Silky? Smooth?

HERBAL TEA

Tea is good for your mind and body — so good that you can literally bathe in it! It is believed by health experts that many herbs have healing properties, from relieving pain (chamomile) to calming your nerves (lavender) to healing your skin (mint). Create your own blend that's perfect for your needs right now.

How to use it: Add loose-leaf tea of your choice to a mesh bag with a drawstring top (found at craft stores). Let it soak for the duration of your bath.

EPSOM SALT

Epsom salt is a special kind of salt that can relax sore muscles and tired feet. Athletes often soak in Epsom salt-filled baths to relieve injuries and soreness. It can be found in the beauty or health aisles of grocery stores. Adding aluminum-free baking soda to your Epsom salt bath can make your skin extra soft.

How to use it: While the bathtub is filling, add one cup of Epsom salt and two cups of baking soda to the water. Soak for about 15 minutes.

BATH OIL

Love essential oils? Bath oils are a great way to add your favorite fragrance to a long soak. See page 126 to learn about the healing benefits of various essential oils. Lavender is an obvious choice for a just-before-bed bath thanks to its calming aroma.

How to use it: Make your own bath oil by mixing five drops of lavender essential oil with a tablespoon of olive oil in a small glass bowl. Stir well. Pour carefully into the water while the bathtub is filling.

Be careful! Oils can make bathtub surfaces slippery. A non-slip bath mat may help. Wipe the bathtub with a dry towel after use.

OATMEAL

Oatmeal can soothe dry, irritated, or itchy skin. That's why it's used so frequently in lotions for sensitive skin. If sensitive skin or allergies are a problem for you, an oatmeal soak might be exactly what your body needs to calm down.

How to use it: In a blender or coffee grinder, grind one cup of rolled or old-fashioned oats into a very fine powder. Or buy colloidal oatmeal, which has already been ground. (Don't use instant oats.) Add while the bathtub is filling.

BATH SALTS

Bath salts combine the healing benefits of salt and essential oil for a great one-two punch. You can also try blending two different kinds of salt (like Epsom and sea salt) or two different essential oils (like lemon and rosemary).

How to use it: Mix five drops of essential oil of your choice with ½ cup coarse sea salt in a small glass bowl. Stir well. Pour carefully into the water while the bathtub is filling.

MILK

Milk isn't just for drinking! It's hydrating, soothing, and may improve your skin health. A milk bath will make the water — and your skin — feel smooth and silky. But don't grab a gallon out of your refrigerator — powdered milk is best for baths.

How to use it: While the bathtub is filling, add one cup of whole powdered milk (found at grocery stores).

"TO FIND YOURSELF, THINK FOR YOURSELF." – SOCRATES

Play Mood Music

MUSIC IS POWERFUL

It can get your muscles moving and boost your mood with just a few notes, and it can toy with your emotions in more ways than one. Slow, classical music can soothe your mind, as well as lower your heart rate, blood pressure, and stress levels. Amazing, right? Here are some ideas for music that can change your mood.

MOZART'S STRING QUINTET NO. 5 IN D MAJOR

Some scientists believe in "the Mozart effect": listening to Mozart for 10 minutes before taking a test may help you get a higher score! Other scientists believe any kind of music will give your brain a temporary boost.

Mindfulness Tip: As you listen to the music, pay attention to the sound of each note. When you notice that you're thinking about something and that the music has faded into the background of your mind, gently turn your attention again to the sound of the music. Enjoy each note.

MOVIE SCORES

The instrumental movie soundtrack, or background music, from your favorite movie might be just what you need when you're looking to relax. *Amélie*, *Grand Budapest Hotel*, *Ever After*, and *Up* are just a few great options.

TCHAIKOVSKY'S BALLET SUITES

Choose from *Swan Lake*, *The Nutcracker*, or *Sleeping Beauty* – all of Pyotr Tchaikovsky's ballet suites are magical. Knowing that someone has danced so gracefully to this music makes you feel lighter than air just listening to it.

"WEIGHTLESS" BY MARCONI UNION

This British band worked with sound therapists to create "the most relaxing song ever." It's eight minutes long, and they don't recommend listening to it while driving. That's how relaxing it is!

WORLD MUSIC

Have you ever tried listening to French jazz? Classic Indian flute? Spanish guitar? Japanese koto music? Every culture around the world creates its own unique sounds. When you listen, you'll feel transported to another place.

ACOUSTIC COVERS

Calming music doesn't have to be instrumental! Acoustic covers of your favorite songs are a great place to start. They're often slower, more mellow versions that are stripped down to just a voice and a guitar or piano.

"WHERE WORDS FAIL, MUSIC SPEAKS." – HANS CHRISTIAN ANDERSEN

Be Prepared

Planning is a strategy for managing — and reducing — stress. In fact, planning ahead has the ability to prevent stress before it even starts!

Being prepared is closely tied to being productive. And when you're prepared and productive, you'll have more free time and less stress, which means you'll be happier. Not bad, huh? Here are some simple ways to plan ahead to make tomorrow — and future tomorrows — go more smoothly.

- PICK OUT TOMORROW'S OUTFIT TONIGHT.

- BEFORE YOU LEAVE SCHOOL ON FRIDAY, LOOK AT NEXT WEEK'S SCHEDULE AND MENTALLY PREPARE.

- CREATE A STUDY SCHEDULE FOR AN UPCOMING TEST.

- PACK YOUR LUNCH AND A SNACK THE NIGHT BEFORE.

- EVERY MORNING, WRITE DOWN THE THREE MOST IMPORTANT THINGS YOU HAVE TO DO THAT DAY.

- SCHEDULE AND STICK TO A BEDTIME (SEE PAGE 138 FOR TIPS). DON'T JUST SET AN ALARM FOR WAKING UP, SET ONE FOR BEDTIME TOO.

- CREATE A WEEKLY AND A DAILY TO-DO LIST.

- START SAVING A SMALL AMOUNT OF MONEY NOW FOR SOMETHING IN THE FUTURE.

- ESTIMATE HOW MUCH TIME YOU THINK YOUR HOMEWORK WILL TAKE EACH NIGHT.

- WHEN PACKING FOR A TRIP, PUT TOGETHER COMPLETE OUTFITS INSTEAD OF RANDOM ITEMS.

- ON SUNDAY NIGHT, MAKE A CHECKLIST FOR THE WHOLE WEEK.

- SET ASIDE TIME EACH DAY TO RELAX, DO YOGA, OR MEDITATE.

- BREAK DOWN A BIG PROJECT INTO SMALLER TASKS AND PLUG THEM INTO YOUR SCHEDULE.

- IF YOU KNOW YOU WON'T HAVE TIME TO GET EVERYTHING DONE, ASK FOR HELP IN ADVANCE.

- DO YOUR LAUNDRY EVERY WEEKEND SO ALL YOUR FAVORITE OUTFITS ARE READY FOR THE WEEK.

- PACK YOUR SCHOOL BAG THE NIGHT BEFORE.

- PLAN A "BUFFER DAY" BETWEEN DUE DATES SO THAT YOU COMPLETE ASSIGNMENTS OR PROJECTS ONE DAY EARLIER THAN NEEDED.

- ORGANIZE YOUR TO-DO LIST BY WHAT'S MOST IMPORTANT.

"BE SO GOOD THEY CAN'T IGNORE YOU." – STEVE MARTIN

Write On

Writing can help you process your experiences and feelings. It can help you deal with stress, anger, loneliness, anxiety, loss, doubt, and more. But you don't have to work through a problem. The act of writing itself can be relaxing, so even fun writing sessions can be good for you. These writing prompts can get you started.

Typing on a computer is OK, but handwriting with a pen and paper is better! It stimulates your brain and keeps you from editing your work.

FREE WRITE

When you wake up in the morning, write three pages. Don't worry about editing your grammar and spelling — just go for it! Write about anything that comes into your mind.

LESSONS LEARNED

Think of something that you are great at — from making new friends to drawing trees to scoring goals in soccer — then explain how you do it to someone else. Write detailed instructions that someone could easily follow.

DREAM BIG

Write about your goals, dreams, and ambitions. As you write, your mood might change for the better. And seeing your dreams written down might inspire you to take action.

HORROR STORY

Feeling self-doubt or fear about a certain challenge that's coming up in your life? Write it out. Write what would happen if your worst fear came true. Now write how you would overcome that worst-case scenario.

WORLD BUILDING

What does a perfect world look like? Create a real or imaginary world that you would love to be a part of. Describe what it looks like, who lives there, and what kind of rules the inhabitants must follow.

SOMEONE ELSE'S SHOES

Step into someone else's life for a moment — a friend, classmate, family member, or a stranger you saw today. Write out what you imagine a day in their life would be like. How is it different from yours?

More on the next page!

SHOW OFF

Write about one of your favorite memories or a big personal accomplishment. Try to remember all the little details like what you wore, what the weather was like, and exactly how you felt. By writing the story, you'll relive the moment — and it will make you happy.

DREAMS DIVULGED

Write about a dream you recently had. Try to fill in any missing gaps, then hypothesize about what it might mean. Was there something in your real life that may have triggered this dream?

THE FUTURE FORETOLD

What will your life be like as an adult? Imagine your career, where you live, what you love to do on a daily basis, and who you love to do it with. Don't hold back! Anything is possible.

EXPLAIN YOURSELF

How would you explain planet Earth to an alien from outer space? Focus on the world as a whole or just your town. What are the most important details that an outsider would need to know about your culture?

Mindfulness Tip: Don't forget to tell them about what it feels like to be there, including smells, sights, and textures.

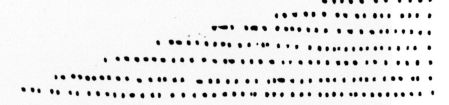

TRAVEL WISH

If you could wake up tomorrow anywhere and during any time period in the history of the world, where would it be? And what would you do once you got there? Write about why you dream of traveling to this place.

SECRET ADMIRER

Write a list of the five people you admire most and why. They can be family members, friends, historical figures, celebrities, or characters from your favorite books or movies. Be sure to explain the exact qualities that make them admirable.

30 BEFORE 30

Make a list of thirty things you want to accomplish before you turn 30. Think about places you'd like to travel, goals you'd like to achieve, people you'd like to meet, and new things you'd like to try.

If you're writing in a journal, keep it in a safe place. Or you can write these exercises on individual sheets of paper and throw them away when you're done. You don't have to keep your writing if you don't want to. The important part is the process, not the product.

Turn the page for more!

FAVORITE THINGS

Make a list of all the things that make you smile – from people to places to things to memories. They can be big or small, real or imaginary. See how close you can get to 100.

DEAR ME

Write a letter to your past or future self. What did you wish you knew or what do you want to know? What have you learned or what do you hope to have learned? How have things changed or how do you hope they'll change?

IF THE WALLS COULD SPEAK

Journal from the point of view of your home, your favorite place, or your school. Imagine all the stories it could tell. Describe how old the building is, the thoughts and feelings it may have, and its likes and dislikes.

LET'S PRETEND

Write about something that's bothering you, but write about it in the third person – as if it happened to someone else. How did they react? How was it different from how you reacted? Did anything turn out differently?

Mindfulness Tip: What would you say to this person that would help them feel better? You can say those words to yourself!

DIVE DEEP

Set a timer for 20 minutes and write about one specific challenge that you had to overcome recently. How did you get through the problem? How did you feel before? What about after? When you're done, analyze why you might have felt that way.

BEST EVER

Write an argument explaining why a certain book, movie, place, or person is your absolute favorite. Pretend that you need to persuade a stranger to believe your point of view. Include as many details as possible.

YESTERDAY

Try to remember everything you did yesterday from the moment you woke up to the moment you went to bed. It's easy to forget about the little details of your everyday life. Document it all here.

LAST MEAL

If you could have only one meal for the rest of your life, what would it be? Describe each choice you made: how it's cooked, how it tastes, and how it makes you feel, as well as where you'd get it and where you'd eat it.

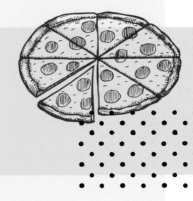

Make a Journal Jar. Write each of these prompts onto a scrap of paper, then fold it and place it in a glass jar. Add your own prompts if you feel inspired. When it's time to start, pick a random prompt. Then get writing!

"EITHER WRITE SOMETHING WORTH READING OR DO SOMETHING WORTH WRITING." – BENJAMIN FRANKLIN

Calming Breakfast Recipes

Breakfast is the first meal of the day, and you might as well start the day with a stress-reducing meal. The following recipes have at least one ingredient that may help you feel ready to tackle the day.

Berry Smoothie

YOU WILL NEED:

1 cup of ice cubes
½ cup blueberries
½ cup raspberries
½ cup sliced strawberries
½ cup vanilla yogurt
¼ cup milk

Berries are a "super food," filled with nutrients and vitamins that can give you a super start to your day. Berries can keep your brain healthy and strong.

Directions:

Mix all ingredients in a blender until smooth. Makes one smoothie.

Cinnamon Honey Oatmeal

YOU WILL NEED:

½ cup old-fashioned oats
1 cup water or milk
pinch of cinnamon
1 tsp honey
1 egg, beaten

You may feel a bit calmer after a cozy bowl of warm oatmeal, which is topped with nutrient-filled honey and cinnamon. Starting your day with a healthy, filling meal means you may feel just a little more ready to tackle whatever comes your way.

Directions:

Make the oatmeal on the stovetop according to the directions on the package. When oatmeal is almost done cooking, stir in egg until oatmeal is smooth and creamy. Finish with a drizzle of honey and a sprinkle of cinnamon.

"YOU MAY HAVE TO FIGHT A BATTLE MORE THAN ONCE TO WIN IT." – MARGARET THATCHER

Power-Up Afternoon Snacks

You are what you eat! So when you need an afternoon pick-me-up, what else would you grab but an energizing snack? The following recipes include ingredients that naturally provide a boost to your body and your mind. Keep a snack in your bag or locker for emergencies, or pre-make some snacks that are easy to grab at home.

Avocado Toast

YOU WILL NEED:

one slice of toast
half an avocado
olive oil
salt
lemon juice

Avocado is filled with stress-relieving B vitamins. Plus it's delicious!

Directions:

Toast a slice of bread. Slice or mash half an avocado and spread it on the toast with a butter knife. Drizzle with olive oil, then sprinkle with salt and a little lemon juice.

Mindfulness Tip: As you bite into the toast, notice the crispiness of the toast, the smoothness of the avocado, and the tartness of the lemon juice. As you chew, pay attention to what happens to these different textures and tastes as they mix together in your mouth.

Protein Pinwheels

YOU WILL NEED:

1 whole-wheat tortilla
hummus
2 slices of turkey deli meat
1 stick mozzarella string cheese

Your body needs protein to build and repair bones, muscles, and more. Turkey and mozzarella cheese are packed with protein. Whole wheat gives you fiber, which helps you feel full.

Directions:

Spread a thin layer of hummus on one side of the tortilla. Layer turkey slices on top. Place the string cheese at one edge and roll the turkey and tortilla around it. Slice the roll of the tortilla with a knife to create pinwheels.

Triple Threat Trail Mix

YOU WILL NEED:

1 cup toasted Os cereal
½ cup almonds
½ cup dried cherries
¼ cup dark chocolate chips
¼ tsp cinnamon

The combination of nuts, cinnamon, and dark chocolate is a powerful mix that may give a boost to your energy and your mood. Cherries add a bit of sweetness and some vitamin C that can help keep you strong.

Directions:

Add ingredients to a bowl and stir. Scoop half-cup servings into resealable plastic bags. Makes about four servings.

YOU WILL NEED:

1 banana
1 cup ice cubes
½ cup oats
½ cup vanilla yogurt
½ cup milk
2 tsp honey
dash of cinnamon (optional)

Power-Up Smoothie

This smoothie is a great energy boost. It's full of fiber, which will keep you feeling full and balanced, so your energy doesn't crash hard later on.

Directions:

Mix all ingredients in a blender until smooth. Makes one smoothie.

"TELL ME WHAT YOU EAT, AND I WILL TELL YOU WHO YOU ARE." – JEAN ANTHELME BRILLAT-SAVARIN

Rearrange Your Room

You could call feng shui (pronounced fung shway) the ancient Chinese art of interior design. It focuses on how to style your room in a way that lets good energy or "chi" flow freely and keeps bad energy out. It's also about finding a harmony between your energy and your home's energy.

Sometimes just switching things up can go a long way toward helping you feel better.

Here are some feng shui principles you can apply to your bedroom:

CHOOSE CALMING COLORS SUCH AS LIGHT BLUES, GREENS, AND LAVENDERS. EARTH TONES SUCH AS CORALS, GRAYS, AND TANS ARE ALSO PEACEFUL.

FIND DECORATIONS WITH SOFT LINES AND CURVES, NOT SHARP CORNERS.

CLEAR AWAY ALL CLUTTER, ESPECIALLY UNDER YOUR BED.

STRIVE FOR BALANCE. A SOFT BLANKET CAN COUNTER THE SHARP EDGES OF A HEADBOARD. A NIGHTSTAND ON EITHER SIDE OF YOUR BED CREATES SYMMETRY.

MOVE YOUR BED DIAGONAL FROM THE DOOR, SO YOU CAN SEE THE DOOR FROM YOUR BED, BUT YOU'RE NOT DIRECTLY IN LINE WITH IT.

HANG A PIECE OF ART THAT YOU LOVE ON THE WALL THAT FACES YOUR BED.

WHEN IT COMES TO YOUR DESK, AVOID FACING A SOLID WALL OR HAVING YOUR BACK TO THE DOOR.

GET RID OF ANY ITEM OR PHOTO THAT CAUSES YOU STRESS, THAT YOU DON'T LIKE, OR THAT BRINGS UP A BAD MEMORY.

Mindfulness Tip: As you try out different arrangements and colors in your room, really pay attention to how you feel. For example, does clearing out clutter make you feel calmer? Do pastel colors make you feel relaxed?

"INACTION BREEDS DOUBT AND FEAR. ACTION BREEDS CONFIDENCE AND COURAGE. IF YOU WANT TO CONQUER FEAR, DO NOT SIT HOME AND THINK ABOUT IT. GO OUT AND GET BUSY." – DALE CARNEGIE

Smile

Your body language and your mood are tied together more directly than you think. Smiling might make you feel happier — even if you're faking it! Some studies suggest that when your lips turn upward, it sends good vibes to your brain that make you think positive thoughts. According to these studies, the more you smile, the more positive your outlook may become.

Go ahead: imagine something that you absolutely love. Think of something that inspires you, makes you laugh, or really wows you. There you go — you're smiling!

SMILING IS A LOT EASIER THAN FROWNING. IT TAKES FEWER MUSCLES TO SMILE THAN IT DOES TO FROWN!

IT'S BEEN SAID THAT SMILING MAKES YOU LIVE LONGER. IT COULD BE BECAUSE SMILING CREATES POSITIVE FEELINGS, WHICH ARE ASSOCIATED WITH LONGER LIVES.

IN JAPAN, THE EMOTICON FOR SMILING IS DIFFERENT AND FOCUSES MORE ON THE EYES: (^_^)

STUDIES HAVE SHOWN THAT A SMILE IS CONTAGIOUS — ONE PERSON'S SMILE CAUSES TWO OTHER PEOPLE TO SMILE!

A TYPICAL FACE CAN CREATE 5,000 DIFFERENT EXPRESSIONS, AND THERE ARE AT LEAST 19 DIFFERENT VERSIONS OF SMILES.

WE ALMOST INSTANTLY ASSOCIATE A SMILE WITH TRUST AND HONESTY.

HUMANS CAN SPOT A SMILE FROM 300 FEET — OR AN ENTIRE FOOTBALL FIELD — AWAY.

THE SMILE IS SAID TO BE THE MOST RECOGNIZED SYMBOL ON THE PLANET.

"WHEN I GET SAD, I STOP BEING SAD AND BE AWESOME INSTEAD. TRUE STORY." – NEIL PATRICK HARRIS

Loving-Kindness Meditation

Loving-kindness simply means a feeling of friendliness, openheartedness, or warmth. People have been practicing this meditation for thousands of years in places like India and Southeast Asia. On the following page is a slight variation from the traditional practice.

Mindfulness Tip: It's OK to adjust the phrases if they don't work for you. For example, some people aren't comfortable with "may you." If that's you, feel free to drop that part of the phrase. Others feel more comfortable saying "May you be at peace" rather than "May you feel safe." Find the words that work for you!

Get into a relaxed position, either sitting or lying down.

Make sure you're in a comfortable position where you won't be disturbed for about 15 or 20 minutes.

Think of someone who makes you smile. This can be anyone – a friend, a little kid you know, even your cat or dog. Anyone who makes you smile when you think of them.

Of course this living being, like all living beings, wants to be happy. Silently and very slowly, repeat some phrases for this living being – thinking about the meaning of the words as you silently say them. Over several minutes, you are taking your time to repeat these phrases.

- "MAY YOU BE HAPPY."
- "MAY YOU FEEL LOVED AND ACCEPTED FOR WHO YOU ARE."
- "MAY YOU FEEL SAFE."

Repeat these phrases until you feel like you have a little bit of a sense of the wish for happiness, love, and safety of this other being.

After repeating these phrases for several minutes, begin letting go of the image of the being who makes you smile. You are bringing to mind an image of yourself as you are sitting or lying here. Now you are repeating silently these same phrases for yourself, taking several minutes to do this.

- "MAY I BE HAPPY."
- "MAY I FEEL LOVED AND ACCEPTED FOR WHO I AM."
- "MAY I FEEL SAFE."

After several minutes, you are letting go of the image of yourself and bringing to mind a "neutral" person. This is someone who you don't have any feelings for one way or the other. It might be someone in one of your classes who you've never thought much about. You are getting a clear image of this person in your mind, and repeating the phrases for them. Remembering to feel the meaning of the words, you are taking your time and doing this slowly.

- "MAY YOU BE HAPPY."
- "MAY YOU FEEL LOVED AND ACCEPTED FOR WHO YOU ARE."
- "MAY YOU FEEL SAFE."

After silently repeating these phrases for several minutes, you are letting go of the image of the neutral person and bringing to mind a "difficult" person. This is someone who annoys you or bothers you in some way. It's best not to choose the most difficult person in your life (at least to start!) but someone who just kind of bugs you. Being a human being, this person also wants to be happy, like all human beings. So now you are taking a few minutes to repeat the phrases silently for them:

- "MAY YOU BE HAPPY."
- "MAY YOU FEEL LOVED AND ACCEPTED FOR WHO YOU ARE."
- "MAY YOU FEEL SAFE."

Check in with yourself about how you feel about any of these people now. Any different?

Listen To Happy Music

One of the fastest ways to change your mood is by changing the tune. Studies have found that when you're looking to improve your mood, turning on some upbeat music is an easy way to get happy fast.

Luckily, being happy has always been in style! This playlist covers six decades of music that will put a smile on your face.

1960s

"You Can't Hurry Love" by The Supremes

"Here Comes the Sun" by The Beatles

"Sugar Sugar" by The Archies

"Jump in the Line (Shake, Señora)"
by Harry Belafonte

"Build Me Up Buttercup" by The Foundations

"I'm a Believer" by The Monkees

"Ain't No Mountain High Enough"
by Marvin Gaye & Tammi Terrell

"Stand by Me" by Ben E. King

1980s

"Walking on Sunshine" by Katrina and the Waves

"I Just Called (To Say I Love You)" by Stevie Wonder

"Footloose" by Kenny Loggins

"I Wanna Dance with Somebody" by Whitney Houston

"Wake Me Up Before You Go-Go" by Wham

"The Way You Make Me Feel" by Michael Jackson

"Dancing with Myself" by Billy Idol

"And She Was" by Talking Heads

"I'm Gonna Be (500 Miles)" by The Proclaimers

"Don't Worry Be Happy" by Bobby McFerrin

2000s

"I Gotta Feeling" by Black Eyed Peas

"Beautiful Day" by U2

"All for You" by Janet Jackson

"Say Hey (I Love You)" by Michael Franti & Spearhead

"Hey Ya!" by OutKast

"Float On" by Modest Mouse

"Dog Days Are Over" by Florence + The Machine

"I Believe in a Thing Called Love" by The Darkness

"I'm Yours" by Jason Mraz

"Dynamite" by Taio Cruz

"Unwritten" by Natasha Bedingfield

1970s

"Take a Chance on Me" by ABBA

"Three Little Birds" by Bob Marley

"Mr. Blue Sky" by Electric Light Orchestra

"Don't Stop" by Fleetwood Mac

"I Can See Clearly Now" by Johnny Nash

"Imagine" by John Lennon

"Superstition" by Stevie Wonder

"One Way or Another" by Blondie

"Just What I Needed" by The Cars

1990s

"Groove Is in the Heart" by Deee-Lite

"Send Me on My Way" by Rusted Root

"MMMBop" by Hanson

"Freedom" by George Michael

"You Gotta Be" by Des'ree

"Over the Rainbow/What a Wonderful World"
by Israel Kamakawiwo'ole

"Everybody's Free (To Wear Sunscreen)"
by Baz Lurhmann

"Only Wanna Be with You" by Hootie &
the Blowfish

2010s

"Happy" by Pharrell Williams

"Uptown Funk" by Bruno Mars

"Wake Me Up" by Avicii

"Best Day of My Life" by American Authors

"Call Me Maybe" by Carly Rae Jepsen

"Get Lucky" by Daft Punk

"All About That Bass" by Meghan Trainor

"We Found Love" by Rihanna

"Burn" by Ellie Goulding

"Demons" by Imagine Dragons

"Safe and Sound" by Capital Cities

Spread Kindness

When you play a role in making other people happy, it's hard to be unhappy yourself. Write positive messages, jokes, or inspirational quotes on note cards or a pad of sticky notes. Carry them around with you, then leave one behind when the moment is right.

The notes are sure to brighten someone's day if you leave them:

ON A MIRROR IN THE BATHROOM AT SCHOOL.
IN THE CENTER OF A POPULAR BOOK OR MAGAZINE AT THE LIBRARY.
ON THE WINDSHIELD OF A CAR.
IN RANDOM LOCKERS AT SCHOOL.
ON A LUNCH TRAY.
ON A SEAT ON THE BUS.

Ideas:

HOPE YOUR DAY IS GOING GREAT!

YOU'RE BEAUTIFUL!

DON'T GIVE UP!

YOU'RE ONE OF A KIND.

SMILE! IT LOOKS GOOD ON YOU.

YOU LOOK GREAT TODAY!

HAVE AN AWESOME DAY.

STAY POSITIVE!

YOU'RE STRONGER THAN YOU THINK.

TOMORROW IS ANOTHER DAY!

KEEP YOUR CHIN UP.

NEVER GIVE UP ON YOUR DREAMS.

Mindfulness Tip:
Notice how you feel when you leave one of these notes. It's a simple way to boost your mood!

IF YOU'RE COMFORTABLE WITH IT, TRY COMPLIMENTING A STRANGER IN PERSON. IT CAN BE SOMETHING SIMPLE, LIKE "WHAT A PRETTY SKIRT!" OR *"Your laugh is infectious."*

"I'VE LEARNED THAT PEOPLE WILL FORGET WHAT YOU SAID, PEOPLE WILL FORGET WHAT YOU DID, BUT PEOPLE WILL NEVER FORGET HOW YOU MADE THEM FEEL." – MAYA ANGELOU

Find a New Hobby

Hobby: Guitar

When it comes to instruments, there are two different paths you can choose: do you want to learn everything there is to know about a new instrument as well as how to read music? Or do you want to learn how to play a song?

To master the technique, sign up for private or group lessons at a local music school like the School of Rock (www. schoolofrock.com). This is a bigger time commitment, but a very rewarding one. For a free option, or if you'd like to memorize a specific song, you can search for tutorials online that teach you how to read guitar tabs and play chords. JustinGuitar.com has tons of free lessons, or you can check out YouTube for learning specific songs.

Challenge: Learn your favorite song and perform it for your family or friends. If you can, sing along as you play! Ask someone to record your performance so you can watch yourself rocking out.

Hobby: Photography

You don't have to have a fancy camera to become a great photographer. Learning a few simple techniques can improve any photo – even a smartphone selfie! If you'd like to learn the science behind lighting, lenses, and editing, sign up for a class at a local photography school or community college.

If you're just looking to learn some tips and tricks to help make your photos great, check out a digital photography book from the library or search for free articles and lessons online. The Photojojo.com blog is a great place to find fun photo projects and cool tips like how to make a cinemagraph.

Challenge: Email your favorite photo to a local printing shop and have the photo printed in a poster size. Ask the printing shop to mount the image onto foam core. Proudly display your masterpiece in your bedroom.

Hobby: Knitting

To start, sign up for a knitting 101 class at a craft store or community center, check out a knitting book from the library, or find a tutorial online. The website knittinghelp.com has lots of free videos.

As a beginner, you'll need to head to the craft store for a few supplies. Pick up an acrylic, light-colored, medium-weight yarn (visually labeled as Sport, DK, or Worsted) as well as wood or bamboo medium-size knitting needles (US needle sizes 6 to 8, between 10 and 12 inches long). They're the easiest materials to start with! Light yarn makes it easier to see your stitches, wood needles hold the yarn better than plastic and aluminum needles (which are slippery), and shorter needles help you have more control.

Challenge: Once you get the hang of knitting, find a pattern for a big project like a blanket for your bed, a scarf for a loved one, or socks, which you can donate to a homeless shelter.

Mindfulness Tip: As you're knitting, see if you can keep your attention on the feel of the needles in your hands and the sound of the needles clicking against each other.

"FIND SOMETHING YOU'RE PASSIONATE ABOUT AND KEEP TREMENDOUSLY INTERESTED IN IT." – JULIA CHILD

Hobby: Cooking

Taking a cooking class with a family member or friend is tons of fun. These classes are a great way to not only learn new recipes but also acquire some basic skills and gain confidence in the kitchen.

Search for a class at a local cooking school, grocery store, or community college. Avoid "demonstration only" classes — that means you don't get to participate. There are cooking classes on everything from pasta making to sushi making to cake baking. Choose whichever sounds most appetizing.

For a free option, check out a cooking book from the library or follow recipes online. The website Learntocook.com has lots of recipes and advice, and YouTube has cooking videos you can follow along with.

Challenge: Make brunch or dinner for your family or friends at home. Double-check that you have all the tools and ingredients before you begin cooking.

Don't forget to take a photo of the finished product!

Mindfulness Tip: Whether you go for a brisk walk or a fast run, notice how your body feels before and after. Do you notice a difference?

Hobby: Running

If you don't consider yourself a natural athlete, that's OK! With practice, you can become a strong runner. Start by walking for 20 minutes three times a week. When you feel comfortable, try a combination of running and walking for one mile. Alternate one to five minutes of jogging with one to two minutes of walking. Each week, increase your mileage by half a mile until you reach 3.5 miles – that's more than a 5K! Congrats!

Websites like mapmyrun.com can help you find a good route in your neighborhood and help you track your distance. Or head to a local park and find a popular trail with mile markers.

Challenge: Sign up for a 5K (3.1 miles), a 10K (6.2 miles), or a half marathon (13.1 miles). From there you can work your way up to a triathlon or a full marathon. There's always another challenge in the running world.

Hobby: Coding

Learning how to code is like learning another language. HTML and CSS are two programming languages you should learn if you'd like to build a website from scratch. Sign up for a class at a local community college or find tutorials online and teach yourself. CodeAcademy.com is a great resource, with a free class called Make a Website.

If you're not interested in coding but you'd like to start a blog, get started with Wordpress.com or Tumblr.com. Both websites are free and easy to use, and you don't have to know how to code to use either of them.

Challenge: Build a website or blog about something you love. It could be a fan site dedicated to your favorite musician, a place to post your best photos or poetry, or a blog that reviews all the breakfast joints in your town.

Choose Joy

You never know when you'll need a boost. This jar is filled with positivity and can be a daily reminder as to why your life is great.

MY JOY jar

START THE DAY WITH A SMILE!

Directions:

YOU WILL NEED:

paper, cut into strips
a marker or pen
a glass jar
stickers, ribbon, and tape

On the strips of paper, write down:

- YOUR HAPPIEST MEMORIES
- QUOTES THAT INSPIRE YOU
- YOUR FAVORITE PLACES
- NICE THINGS PEOPLE HAVE SAID ABOUT YOU
- QUOTES FROM YOUR FAVORITE BOOKS OR MOVIES
- AMAZING THINGS YOU'VE ACCOMPLISHED
- RANDOM THINGS THAT MAKE YOU SMILE
- INSIDE JOKES THAT MAKE YOU LAUGH
- SONG LYRICS THAT SPEAK TO YOU

Fold the paper slips and place them inside the jar. Decorate the outside of the jar with stickers, colorful ribbon, or washi tape.

When you're feeling down, grab a strip of paper and keep it with you throughout the day as a reminder. Whenever something makes you happy, write it down and add it to the jar!

Mindfulness Tip: Notice how you feel when you read one of the strips of paper. Those memories are with you always!

"ONLY IN THE DARKNESS CAN YOU SEE THE STARS."
- MARTIN LUTHER KING JR.

Give Thanks

A handwritten thank-you note is a small gesture that says a lot. And the simple act of writing one does a lot for your body and mind. When you choose to be thankful and gracious, it means you're choosing not to be jealous or envious. And it means you're choosing to be a healthier, happier person.

In this instance, being thankful is not about making yourself feel better — it's about making someone else feel better! Thank-you notes are the easiest way to express gratitude to a friend or family member. It can be an "I was just thinking about you" note or a special thanks for something in particular, but be sure to end it with a resounding thank you . . . for being a reliable friend, a great mentor, an inspiration, or a source of humor and joy.

Here are some simple ways to say thank you in a card:

- I APPRECIATE YOU SO MUCH.
- YOU MEAN THE WORLD TO ME.
- THANK YOU FOR ALL THAT YOU HAVE DONE FOR ME.
- YOU MADE ME FEEL SPECIAL.
- I'M SO LUCKY TO HAVE A FRIEND LIKE YOU.
- YOU ALWAYS GO ABOVE AND BEYOND.
- I LOOK UP TO YOU SO MUCH.
- YOU HAVE NO IDEA HOW MUCH YOU MEAN TO ME.
- THANK YOU FOR BEING IN MY LIFE.
- I CAN NEVER THANK YOU ENOUGH.
- YOU ARE SO GENEROUS.
- THANK YOU FOR ALWAYS BEING THERE FOR ME.
- YOU READ MY MIND.

- I WILL BE FOREVER GRATEFUL.
- OUR FRIENDSHIP IS A GIFT I WILL ALWAYS TREASURE.
- YOU MADE MY DAY.
- I ADMIRE ALL THAT YOU DO.
- YOU'RE ALWAYS SO THOUGHTFUL.
- YOU HELPED ME MORE THAN YOU KNOW.
- I'M TOUCHED BY THE SUPPORT YOU'VE GIVEN ME.
- YOU'RE THE BEST.
- THANK YOU FOR BEING AWESOME.
- YOU DESERVE MORE THAN JUST A THANK YOU.
- I CHERISH OUR FRIENDSHIP.
- YOU ALWAYS PUT A SMILE ON MY FACE.

Write a card today.

"FEELING GRATITUDE AND NOT EXPRESSING IT IS LIKE WRAPPING A PRESENT AND NOT GIVING IT." – WILLIAM ARTHUR WARD

Be Colorful

Color sparks emotion, and you can use color theory to give a boost to your wardrobe. When you wake up in the morning, think about what you want to accomplish. Pick out an outfit that reflects your goals through its colors. For instance, if you have a busy day at school with tests, presentations, and after-school commitments, you might want to wear blue tones to help you keep calm and be productive. Or maybe you'll decide to wear purple tones to channel a drive for success and promote balance. The choice is yours! On the next page, read about some common colors and the feelings that are associated with them.

Blue

Can increase productivity, create a sense of security, and encourage calmness.

Restful Serene Wise Loyal Focused Authoritative Orderly Peaceful Reflective Sad Balanced Trusting Intelligent Mature Confident Accepting

Green

Symbolizes health, can help alleviate depression, and promotes relaxation.

Natural Cool Growing Healthy Envious Tranquil Harmonized Adventuresome Faithful Lazy Refreshing Safe Sincere Youthful Quiet Calm

Purple

Encourages harmony, can be soothing, and represents success.

Creative Royal Wealthy Sophisticated Wise Exotic Ambitious Respectful Mysterious Sorrowful Intelligent Knowledgeable Secretive Dramatic Beautiful Vain

Yellow

Mentally stimulating, can encourage communication, and is attention-grabbing.

Happy Warm Optimistic Intense Energetic Confident Powerful Playful Warning Inspiring Creative Forgiving Uncertain Innovative Hopeful

Red

Can increase heart rate, create urgency, and encourage strong emotions.

Loving Warm Comforting Exciting Energetic Intense Passionate Devoted Victorious Angry Commanding Courageous Dangerous Desirous Romantic

Orange

Promotes excitement, can show caution, and is seen overall as friendly.

Stimulating Happy Energetic Enthusiastic Warm Action-packed Fun Joyful Generous Prosperous Sophisticated Celebratory Humorous Enduring Strong

If you want to feel more confident before you give a speech, dress in a color that will make you feel strong: orange!

Start a Gratitude Journal

Scientists agree: expressing gratitude is a good thing. Studies have found that it improves your physical and mental health. It also may help you think more positively, since you'll begin focusing on all the good things and the great people that are a part of your life. Starting your journal will help you incorporate gratitude into your daily habits.

To begin, set aside at least five minutes before you go to bed each night to reflect on your day and write down something for which you feel grateful. Your entry can be as simple as expressing gratitude for a positive interaction with a friend. Or you can go into more detail and share the many reasons you feel particularly grateful for that friend.

EVERY DAY

All you need is a dedicated notebook. Keep it by your bed so you remember to write in it each night.

When you're feeling down, flip through some old entries. You'll find it hard not to smile.

Here are some tips for making your gratitude journal great:

- TO GET STARTED, THINK ABOUT THE BEST PART OF YOUR DAY OR THE WEEK.

- FOCUS ON PEOPLE, NOT THINGS. WRITE ABOUT THE POSITIVE INTERACTIONS YOU HAD WITH FRIENDS AND FAMILY — EVEN THE LITTLEST OF MOMENTS MATTER.

- WRITE DOWN WHAT HAPPENED AND WHY YOU ARE GRATEFUL. IMAGINE WHAT LIFE WOULD BE LIKE *WITHOUT* THAT MOMENT OR THAT PERSON. THAT MIGHT HELP YOU DESCRIBE HOW GRATEFUL YOU ARE.

- IF YOU WRITE ABOUT YOUR OWN ACHIEVEMENT, ELABORATE ON HOW YOU GREW AS YOU WORKED TOWARD THIS GOAL. DON'T FOCUS ONLY ON THE GOAL ITSELF.

- IF YOU'VE HAD A CHALLENGING DAY OR WEEK, FOCUS ON WHAT YOU LEARNED FROM THESE CHALLENGES.

- SOME ENTRIES MAY BE MORE ELABORATE THAN OTHERS. MAYBE AN AFTERNOON SNACK WAS THE THING YOU WERE MOST THANKFUL FOR TODAY. THAT'S ALL RIGHT!

- YOU DON'T HAVE TO STICK WITH JUST WRITING — YOU CAN DOODLE OR TREAT YOUR JOURNAL LIKE A SCRAPBOOK, ATTACHING PHOTOS, TICKET STUBS, AND MORE.

"ENJOY THE LITTLE THINGS IN LIFE BECAUSE ONE DAY YOU'LL LOOK BACK AND REALIZE THEY WERE THE BIG THINGS." – KURT VONNEGUT

Laugh

Laughing is good for you! One good "ha!" can relax your muscles and relieve stress for up to 45 minutes. It will make you happier by countering depressing or anxious thoughts, and it can make you healthier. When repeated over a long period of time, negative thoughts may stress your immune system, while positive ones can strengthen it. Amazing, right? Laughter really is the best medicine.

Knock knock.
Who's there?
Interrupting cow.
Interrupting c—
MOO!

Did you hear about the mathematician who's afraid of negative numbers? He'll stop at nothing to avoid them.

What do you call a song about a tortilla?
A wrap.

Turn on one of these flicks and you'll be sure to get your required daily dose of humor.

PRINCESS BRIDE	GUARDIANS OF THE GALAXY	THE LION KING
ELF	NEVER BEEN KISSED	NAPOLEON DYNAMITE
BACK TO THE FUTURE	HOOK	FINDING NEMO
SHREK	BRING IT ON	PITCH PERFECT
FATHER OF THE BRIDE	JUMANJI	MISS CONGENIALITY
FREAKY FRIDAY	13 GOING ON 30	MAMMA MIA!
SHE'S ALL THAT	MRS. DOUBTFIRE	TEEN WITCH
HOME ALONE	THE LEGO MOVIE	UP
INSIDE OUT	FERRIS BUELLER'S DAY OFF	CLUELESS
THE INCREDIBLES	BABE	SHE'S THE MAN
10 THINGS I HATE ABOUT YOU	THE PRINCESS DIARIES	ADVENTURES IN BABYSITTING
GOONIES	THE PARENT TRAP (1998)	SIXTEEN CANDLES
ELLA ENCHANTED	E.T.	GREASE
LEGALLY BLONDE	THE SECRET LIFE OF PETS	BEND IT LIKE BECKHAM
TOY STORY	GIRLS JUST WANT TO HAVE FUN	

What does a nosey pepper do?
Get jalapeño business.

What did the ocean say to the beach?
Nothing. It just waved.

What did the pirate say on his 80th birthday?
"Aye, Matey!"

"A DAY WITHOUT LAUGHTER IS A DAY WASTED." – CHARLIE CHAPLIN

Volunteer

People who volunteer often say their stress levels are lower, they're happier, and they feel healthier. Volunteering can also help you feel more connected to others, which fights off feelings of loneliness. The results are almost instantaneous — you'll feel so great helping others that you won't want to stop.

DoSomething.org and VolunteerMatch.org are two great resources with lots of unique volunteer opportunities that can be tailored to your passions.

Here are some volunteer opportunities that are worth looking into.

HELP THE HUNGRY

Food banks are always looking for help sorting, packing, and stacking donated food items that they then give to pantries and shelters. Homeless shelters are often looking for help to serve meals throughout the year and on holidays. These are great opportunities for a group of family or friends. Find more information at **feedingamerica.org** or **homelessshelterdirectory.org.**

ASSIST A NEIGHBOR

Help mow the lawn, shovel snow, take out the trash, or rake leaves for an elderly neighbor. While daily errands can be a challenge, people of advanced age often suffer from loneliness too. Make a weekly date to spend time playing board games with an older neighbor or spend an afternoon chatting with residents at a local nursing home or senior center.

CHEER ON THE COMPETITION

Marathons and run/walks always need help passing out water and snacks and cheering on the runners. They're often raising awareness and money for a good cause. Standing on the sidelines will get your adrenaline pumping — and it might inspire you to sign up as a participant next year!

SUPPORT THE TROOPS

Deployed soldiers (the men and women who are fighting for our country overseas) love to receive notes and care packages throughout the year. Veterans, first responders, and wounded heroes also deserve thanks. Find more information at **soldiersangels.org** or **operationgratitude.com.**

GIVE BACK TO NATURE

Parks are wonderful, and it takes a lot of effort to keep them clean, groomed, and safe. The U.S. National Park Service and the U.S. Forest Service have lots of volunteer opportunities. In fact, some of their youth volunteer programs double as summer jobs. Your local park district may also organize chances to volunteer on Earth Day and other holidays. Find more information at **nps.gov** or **volunteer.gov.**

Find a Furry Friend

Furry friends of all shapes and sizes make you happier by giving you physical contact, providing a fun distraction, and reducing your stress. Animals offer unconditional love and support — with no judgment! — which can help you heal and can cheer you up. Even if you don't have a pet at home, there are ways to incorporate animals into your life.

Mindfulness Tip: Whether it's your pet or an animal in a petting zoo or park, take time to just observe the animal. If you notice that your mind starts to drift as you are watching, gently bring your attention back to watching the animal.

- LOOK AT CUTE PHOTOS OF BABY ANIMALS ON THE INTERNET. YES, EVEN PHOTOS CAN MAKE US HAPPIER! TRY ZOOBORNS.COM OR CHECK OUT LIVE WEBCAMS FROM ZOOS AROUND THE WORLD.

- READ A BOOK OR TAKE A NAP WITH YOUR PET SNUGGLED CLOSELY TO YOU.

- IF YOU DON'T HAVE A PET, OFFER TO WALK A NEIGHBOR'S DOG OR CAT-SIT WHILE THEY'RE ON VACATION.

- VISIT A PETTING ZOO. THE ACT OF PETTING AN ANIMAL CAN MAKE YOU FEEL HAPPIER!

- GOOGLE "PHOTO-BOMBING ANIMALS." NOT ONLY ARE ANIMALS CUTE, THEY'RE HILARIOUS TOO!

- VOLUNTEER AT YOUR LOCAL ANIMAL SHELTER.

- IF YOUR FAMILY IS WILLING, VOLUNTEER TO FOSTER A DOG OR CAT. THAT MEANS YOU TEMPORARILY HOUSE A PET UNTIL IT FINDS A "FOREVER HOME."

- THERE'S NOTHING BETTER THAN A DOG PARK ON A SATURDAY MORNING. WATCH NEW FRIENDSHIPS BEING FORMED — YOU MIGHT MAKE SOME YOURSELF!

- SIGN UP FOR A HORSEBACK RIDING CLASS OR AN EQUESTRIAN TOUR OF A NEARBY TRAIL OR PARK. YOU'LL MAKE FAST FRIENDS WITH YOUR RIDE!

- READ A BOOK ABOUT AN ANIMAL OF YOUR CHOICE.

Here are some good options:

→ *WHITE FANG* BY JACK LONDON

→ *BLACK BEAUTY* BY ANNA SEWELL

→ *THE LIFE OF PI* BY YANN MARTEL

→ *BECAUSE OF WINN DIXIE* BY KATE DICAMILLO

→ *THE MUSIC OF DOLPHINS* BY KAREN HESSE

→ *HOOT* BY CARL HIAASEN

→ *PLAIN KATE* BY ERIN BOW

"ANIMALS ARE SUCH AGREEABLE FRIENDS — THEY ASK NO QUESTIONS, THEY PASS NO CRITICISMS." – GEORGE ELIOT

Make a Worry Box

Are you a worrywart? If you have a big imagination, a simple worry can turn into an elaborate — and exaggerated — threat. This kind of stress isn't good for your body. Too much worry can have a big effect on your body, from increasing your heart rate to giving you a headache or stomachache.

Here's one way to help lessen the impact of things that are bothering you: store them away! A worry box is a special place to keep your concerns. Simply write down your worry on a slip of paper and then put it in the box. At the end of the month, empty the box and discard all your worries. Or, if you're brave enough, you can read through them. You may find that some of these thoughts took care of themselves . . . and that you had nothing to sweat about!

YOU WILL NEED:

box
wrapping paper
scissors
tape
stickers (optional)
markers (optional)

Directions:

Use wrapping paper to cover the box as you would with a present. Cut a hole at the top of the box. This is where you'll deposit your worries. Decorate with stickers or markers.

Mindfulness Tip: You are free to take them out and look at your worries whenever you want, but having a box for them helps you put them aside so that you don't have to think about them constantly.

"WORRY NEVER ROBS TOMORROW OF ITS SORROW, IT ONLY SAPS TODAY OF ITS JOY." – LEO BUSCAGLIA

Treat Yourself

Sometimes you need a treat — and this single-serve cupcake recipe will do just the trick. It's a party for one. The reason? Because you said so!

Cupcake for One

YOU WILL NEED:

3 tbsp flour
1 tbsp sugar
¼ tsp baking powder
1 tbsp oil
1 tbsp milk
¼ tsp vanilla extrac

Directions:

Preheat oven to 350 degrees Fahrenheit. Mix ingredients together in a small bowl. Pour into a cupcake liner in a muffin tin. Bake for 15-18 minutes. Let cupcake cool.

Frosting

YOU WILL NEED:

1 tbsp butter (at room temperature)
¼ tsp vanilla extract
2 tbsp powdered sugar
sprinkles

Directions:

Mix ingredients together in a small bowl. (Mash butter with a fork if it's too firm.) Once your cupcake has cooled to room temperature, use a butter knife to spread a thin layer of frosting onto the cupcake. Top with sprinkles.

"WE MUST BE OUR OWN BEFORE WE CAN BE ANOTHER'S."
– RALPH WALDO EMERSON

Break a Sweat

Exercise has been proven to make you happy. And it can make you feel more confident, help you fall asleep at night, and suppress anxiety. The list goes on and on! It almost sounds too good to be true. But the reality is this: after a workout, you'll be more productive and you'll probably have a more positive outlook. On the following pages is a 20-minute routine you can do in the comfort of your own home.

Take a break whenever you need it. Listen to your body!

WHEN DOING CORE EXERCISES, SUCH AS THE ALTERNATING REACH, ELBOW PLANK, AND SIDE PLANK, MAKE SURE TO KEEP YOUR ABDOMINAL MUSCLES TIGHTENED THROUGHOUT. THIS WILL HELP PROTECT YOUR BACK FROM ANY STRAIN.

YOU WILL NEED:

a jump rope
a yoga mat
a stopwatch or clock

MINUTES 0:00–4:00: JUMP ROPE

Jumping is a great full-body workout that gets your heart pumping. To make sure the jump rope is the correct length, place one foot on the center of the rope. Pull the handles up. They should reach your armpits. The best place to jump rope is on a hard surface.

· Single jump with your feet together for 30 seconds.

· For the next 30 seconds, alternate jumping a few inches forward then a few inches backward.

· Rest for 30 seconds. Walk around and grab a small sip of water if you need it. Don't sit.

· Single jump with one foot at a time (like you're running in place) for 30 seconds.

· For the next 30 seconds, alternate jumping a few inches to the left, then a few inches to the right with your legs together.

· Rest for 30 seconds. Walk around and grab a small sip of water if you need it. Don't sit.

· Single jump with one foot at a time (like you're running in place) for 30 seconds.

· For the last 30 seconds, alternate jumping with your feet together and your feet apart (like a jumping jack) for 30 seconds.

MINUTE 4:00–5:00: ALTERNATING REACH

Get on all fours with your wrists directly underneath your shoulders and your knees directly underneath your hips. Now slowly raise and straighten the left arm and the right leg. Repeat with right arm and left leg. Alternate for the next minute.

MINUTE 5:00–6:00: ELBOW PLANK

With your elbows directly underneath your shoulders, get into a push-up position but keep your forearms on the ground. Hold for one minute or as long as you can without your knees touching the ground.

MINUTE 6:00–7:00: SIDE PLANK

From the plank position, twist your body to the left as you raise your left arm straight up. Hold for 30 seconds. Repeat on right side.

MINUTES 7:00–11:00: JUMP ROPE

Repeat the routine from the previous page.

MINUTE 11:00–11:30: SCISSOR KICKS

Lie on your back. Keep your lower back on the ground throughout, and tighten your abs. Slowly lift your left leg. Now slowly lower your left leg while slowly raising your right leg. Keep your legs as straight as possible and try to keep your heels off the floor. Repeat for 30 seconds.

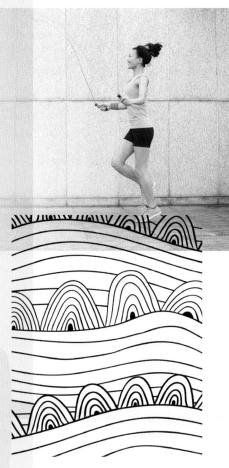

MINUTE 11:30–12:00: SITTING TWISTS

Sit up with your legs straight in front you. Lean slightly backward with a straight back and lift and bend your knees so you're balancing on your bottom. Clasp your hands together. Twist your upper body and tap the floor on your left side. Repeat on the right. Alternate. Do as many as you can in 30 seconds.

MINUTE 12:00–12:30: SQUAT JUMPS

With your legs a little wider than your shoulders and your toes pointing slightly outward, sit back into a squat position. As you rise back up, jump and straighten your legs. Land lightly on your feet in a squat position. Repeat. Do as many as you can in 30 seconds.

MINUTE 12:30–13:00: WALKING LUNGES

Stand with your feet together and hands on your hips. Step forward with your right leg into a lunge position. Bring your feet back together by moving your left leg to your right. Now repeat on the left side. Alternate for 30 seconds.

MINUTES 13:00–15:00: REPEAT

Repeat the series of four exercises from minutes 11:00 to 13:00.

MINUTES 15:00–19:00: JUMP ROPE

Repeat the first three minutes of the routine on page 111, then march lightly in place for a minute.

MINUTE 19:00–19:30: COBRA POSE

Lie on your stomach as if you're ready to begin a push-up. Now slowly raise only your upper body. Your thighs and feet remain flat on the ground. You should feel the stretch in your stomach and back. Make sure your arms are straight and your shoulders are relaxed.

MINUTE 19:30–20:00: DOWNWARD-FACING DOG

From Cobra position, lower your upper body back to the ground. Push yourself up into a plank, then lean back into your heels and push your hips into the sky to create an inverted V. Your arms and legs should be straight. Try to press your heels toward the ground.

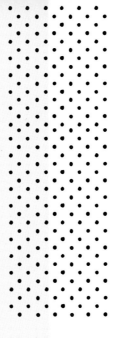

Mindfulness Tip: As you hold this pose, notice sensations arising throughout your body.

Breathe.

113

Have a Vision

Vision boards, or dream boards, can be hung in your room and can inspire you on a daily basis to keep working toward your goals. Think of each image as a seed that you're planting. One day it will grow into the dream you want to achieve. An everyday reminder encourages you to take action and "water" the seeds you've planted.

Make a Vision Board

What should you put on a vision board? Anything you'd like! Motivational quotes or sayings, words that are important to you, photos that make you happy, people that inspire you, mementos from your favorite places, the goals you want to reach . . . the list goes on and on!

YOU WILL NEED:

images
scissors
glue
shadow box, corkboard, or poster board

Directions

1. Gather the materials you'd like to showcase on your vision board. It's best if you can find images that express your goals, emotions, and dreams as opposed to just words. Print designs or photos off of the Internet, cut out images or words from magazines, write out your favorite quotes or sayings, or include photos and mementos of your own.

2. Now glue the items to your board. Let the vision board dry overnight.

3. Display it on your desk, a nightstand, or another place that you'll see every day. Spend five minutes every day (in the morning or at night) getting inspired by your board.

"CREATE THE HIGHEST, GRANDEST VISION POSSIBLE FOR YOUR LIFE, BECAUSE YOU BECOME WHAT YOU BELIEVE." – OPRAH WINFREY

30-Day Challenge

Declaring a goal is the easy part. Figuring out how to get there — and sticking to it — takes some serious skill. After all, lots of people are great at making to-do lists, but not everyone is great at getting them done. That's the goal of this challenge:

Get things done!

S	M	T	W	T	F	S
					1	2
3	4	5	6	7	8	9
10	11	12	13	14	15	16
17	18	19	20	21	22	23
24	25	26	27	28	29	30

For the next 30 days, you'll tackle a small goal one day at a time. By the end of month, your goal will be achieved! What's one small goal you'd love to reach? Write it down. Then follow these steps:

1. BREAK THE GOAL INTO SMALL STEPS. ASK YOURSELF, WHAT DO I NEED TO DO TO REACH MY GOAL OVER THE NEXT FOUR WEEKS? FOR EXAMPLE, IF YOUR GOAL IS TO WRITE A SHORT STORY, YOU COULD TURN IT INTO A FOUR-STEP PROCESS: BRAINSTORM AN IDEA, MAKE AN OUTLINE, WRITE THE FIRST DRAFT, AND REVISE THE FINAL DRAFT.

2. SET DEADLINES FOR EACH STEP OVER THE NEXT 30 DAYS. STICK TO THEM! USE SOME OF THE GAMIFICATION TRICKS ON PAGE 148 TO HELP YOU STAY FOCUSED.

3. TRACK YOUR PROGRESS. WRITE YOUR DEADLINES IN A TO-DO LIST FORMAT AND CROSS OFF EACH ONE THAT YOU MEET.

If you aren't sure where to begin, check out these ideas for your 30-day challenge:

READ ONE BOOK PER WEEK

LEARN HOW TO PLAY A SONG ON THE GUITAR OR PIANO

WRITE A SHORT STORY

DO A RANDOM ACT OF KINDNESS 30 DAYS IN A ROW

REORGANIZE AND REDECORATE YOUR BEDROOM

WORK OUT THREE DAYS A WEEK FOR THE NEXT MONTH

BRING A LUNCH TO SCHOOL EVERY DAY FOR THE NEXT MONTH

WORK YOUR WAY UP TO A 5K RUN

When you share your goals with others, they feel more real. And you're more likely to stick to them if you know someone else is watching.

"ANYTHING'S POSSIBLE IF YOU'VE GOT ENOUGH NERVE."
- J.K. ROWLING

Start a Nature Journal

A nature journal is a bit more scientific than a traditional diary. It's all about observing the world around you and documenting what you see, think, and feel. All you'll need is a pencil and a blank, unlined journal, preferably hardcover and spiral-bound to make it easy to write on the go. When it comes to nature journaling, you'll want to do it on location in the moment, not later at home.

Mindfulness Tip: When you observe flowers, trees, plants, or other things in nature, really look closely. And once you think you've seen everything, look again. There's always more to see!

Start your nature journal by dating the entry with a location and time. Then start observing: a local park, nature reserve, zoo, or trail — even your own backyard will do. When you're ready, fill the pages with . . .

SKETCHES OR WATERCOLOR PAINTINGS OF PLANTS, FLOWERS, TREES, LANDSCAPES, INSECTS, BIRDS, AND ANIMALS

DESCRIPTIONS OF WEATHER, PATTERNS, SMELLS, AND SOUNDS

OBSERVATIONS ON HOW THE CHANGE OF SEASONS IS AFFECTING A SPECIFIC PLACE

PRESSED FLOWERS AND LEAVES

REFLECTIONS ON HOW NATURE AFFECTS YOUR MOOD AND EMOTIONS

PERSONAL PHOTOGRAPHS OF NATURE

STORIES, POEMS, OR NOTES ABOUT THE NATURAL WORLD

NOTES FROM A DAY HIKE, CAMPING TRIP, OR VACATION

QUESTIONS AND TOPICS YOU'D LIKE TO RESEARCH WHEN YOU GET HOME

Nature journals keep you curious, encourage you to learn, and force you to slow down and reflect. Appreciate the amazing beauty around you, then document your favorite moments. With a little time and effort, your nature journal can become a beautiful keepsake you can flip through when your mood needs a boost.

To press flowers, collect fallen petals or leaves and then place them between two scraps of parchment paper. Set a heavy book on top for a few days until the flowers or petals lie completely flat. Tape or glue the final product into your nature journal.

"ADOPT THE PACE OF NATURE: HER SECRET IS PATIENCE."
— RALPH WALDO EMERSON

Get Inspired

Write down some of your favorite lyrics for your vision board on page 114.

Feeling stuck? Scared? Blue? Bored? You need a boost. Music stimulates a part of your brain that's tied to emotion, which is why music can affect your mood. Pop on one of these tunes when you need a little inspiration. The lyrics are especially motivating. Some will get your feet tapping, while others will ignite a fire inside you. It's hard to walk away from a five-minute dance party or sing-along session without feeling a little bit more awesome.

Here are some tried-and-true songs that are perfect for a pump-up playlist.

"GIRL ON FIRE" BY ALICIA KEYS

"ARE YOU GONNA GO MY WAY" BY LENNY KRAVITZ

"TITANIUM" BY DAVID GUETTA FT. SIA

"WHAT A FEELING" BY IRENE CARA

"SKYSCRAPER" BY DEMI LOVATO

"MAN IN THE MIRROR" BY MICHAEL JACKSON

"BRAVE" BY SARA BAREILLES

"SHAKE IT OFF" BY TAYLOR SWIFT

"FIREWORK" BY KATY PERRY

"SURVIVOR" BY DESTINY'S CHILD

"DEFYING GRAVITY" BY IDINA MENZEL

"I'M COMING OUT" BY DIANA ROSS

"FIGHTER" BY CHRISTINA AGUILERA

"BREAK FREE" BY ARIANA GRANDE FT. ZEDD

"WE WILL ROCK YOU" BY QUEEN

"RIGHT NOW" BY VAN HALEN

"STRONGER" BY BRITNEY SPEARS

"I WILL SURVIVE" BY GLORIA GAYNOR

"EYE OF THE TIGER" BY SURVIVOR

"THE CLIMB" BY MILEY CYRUS

"LIGHTS" BY ELLIE GOULDING

"IT'S MY LIFE" BY BON JOVI

"ROAR" BY KATY PERRY

"SWEET NOTHING" BY CALVIN HARRIS FT. FLORENCE WELCH

"ROLLING IN THE DEEP" BY ADELE

"ONE MORE TIME" BY DAFT PUNK

"RUN THE WORLD (GIRLS)" BY BEYONCÉ

"STRONGER (WHAT DOESN'T KILL YOU)" BY KELLY CLARKSON

"MUSIC CAN CHANGE THE WORLD BECAUSE IT CAN CHANGE PEOPLE." – BONO

Practice Good Posture

Body language is important — and the way you sit and stand is one of the loudest ways your body speaks to others. Standing proud makes you look more confident and feel more confident too. According to some studies, good posture can put you in a good mood. So enough with the slouching!

If you're not sure if your posture is perfect, practice in front of a mirror and look at yourself from different angles. See the difference?

Good Standing Posture

PULL YOUR SHOULDERS BACK AND SLIGHTLY PUFF OUT YOUR CHEST.

YOUR STOMACH SHOULD BE PULLED SLIGHTLY INWARD.

KEEP YOUR HEAD LEVEL AND YOUR EARS IN LINE WITH YOUR SHOULDERS.

YOUR FEET SHOULD BE SHOULDER-WIDTH APART.

MAKE SURE YOUR KNEES ARE "SOFT," NOT LOCKED.

PLACE MOST OF YOUR WEIGHT ON THE BALLS OF YOUR FEET.

Good Sitting Posture

YOUR FEET SHOULD REST FLAT ON THE FLOOR AND YOUR THIGHS SHOULD BE PARALLEL TO THE GROUND. IF THEY'RE NOT, FIND A SEAT THAT'S TALLER OR SHORTER.

PRETEND A STRING IS ATTACHED TO THE CENTER OF YOUR HEAD AND IS BEING PULLED UP.

KEEP YOUR HEAD LEVEL AND YOUR EARS IN LINE WITH YOUR SHOULDERS.

RELAX YOUR SHOULDERS. DON'T LET THEM SCRUNCH UP TO YOUR EARS.

Mindfulness Tip: Notice how you feel as you stand up straight. Do you feel a bit better about yourself? And then notice how you feel when you slouch. What changes?

Another easy way to display confidence is to make and keep eye contact. Try it! You'll get better with practice.

"OPTIMISM IS THE FAITH THAT LEADS TO ACHIEVEMENT. NOTHING CAN BE DONE WITHOUT HOPE AND CONFIDENCE." – HELEN KELLER

Treat Someone Else

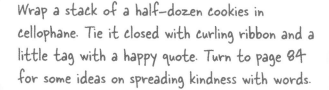

Wrap a stack of a half-dozen cookies in cellophane. Tie it closed with curling ribbon and a little tag with a happy quote. Turn to page 84 for some ideas on spreading kindness with words.

Tackling a new recipe is a rewarding challenge on its own. But the great thing about this recipe is that you get to share it with others. In fact, that's the most important part of this activity. Bake up a batch of these soft and chewy chocolate chip cookies, then share them with a friend, neighbor, teacher, or even your own family.

Chocolate Chip Cookies

YOU WILL NEED:
2 ½ cups flour
1 tsp baking soda
½ tsp salt
1 ½ cup brown sugar
1 cup butter
1 tsp vanilla extract
2 eggs
½ cup dark chocolate chips

Directions:

Preheat oven to 400 degrees Fahrenheit.

Combine the flour, baking soda, and salt in a medium-size bowl. Using a mixer, blend butter, sugar, and vanilla in a large bowl. Beat in eggs, then slowly add the flour mixture. Once combined, add chocolate chips.

Place heaping tablespoon-sized scoops evenly on a cookie sheet. Top each scoop with a few more chocolate chips. Bake for 6 to 7 minutes so the edges are brown but the center is still very soft. Let cool for at least 5 minutes before using a spatula to remove from cookie sheet.

Makes about 20 cookies.

Choose dark chocolate chips instead of milk or semi-sweet. Dark chocolate has many health benefits and even encourages your brain to release endorphins, which make you happy!

"NO ACT OF KINDNESS, NO MATTER HOW SMALL, IS EVER WASTED." – AESOP

Aromatherapy

Many scientists believe that scents can affect your mood. Imagine the smell of warm chocolate chip cookies right out of the oven, freshly cut grass on a sunny summer morning, or just-washed sheets as you sink into your bed at night.

In aromatherapy, fragrant essential oils are said to naturally influence our mind, body, and spirit. They're not guaranteed to make you feel a certain way, but they definitely smell great. The scents are natural — like lemon, vanilla, or lavender. Sadly, you won't find a chocolate chip cookie essential oil. (Wouldn't that be nice?)

Mindfulness Tip: When you use these essential oils, take a moment to slowly breathe in and really appreciate the aroma.

Here are some commonly used essential oils and their potential benefits:

PEPPERMINT

Energy boosting, invigorating, and promotes concentration.
Good for: when you need to study for a test

LEMON

Energy boosting, induces alertness, and cleansing.
Good for: when you're feeling run down

VANILLA

Relaxing, promotes joy and happiness.
Good for: when you want to start your day off right

LAVENDER

Calming, soothing, and tension relieving.
Good for: when you're feeling stressed

JASMINE

Revitalizing, confidence inducing, and fatigue fighting.
Good for: when you're feeling blue

CINNAMON

Mind sharpening, immunity boosting, and tension relieving.
Good for: when you need to focus

ROSEMARY

Stimulating, pain and anxiety relieving, and clarity inducing.
Good for: when you're exhausted, mentally or physically

ROMAN CHAMOMILE

Soothing, anxiety relieving, and gentle.
Good for: when you're sore, worn down, or anxious

ORANGE

Mood-boosting, stimulating, and cleansing.
Good for: when you're disorganized, frustrated, or overwhelmed

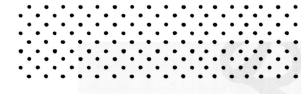

Essential oils should not be used by children under the age of six. Never apply essential oils directly to your skin. Instead, create one of the projects on page 129 or 137.

You can purchase lotions, candles, and perfumes that are made from your favorite essential oils. Or you can create your own concoctions. Essential oils can be found at health food stores or online.

SCENTED LOTION

Add your favorite essential oil to unscented hand or face lotion, three to six drops per ounce. Be sure to blend well and store in a clean, lidded glass jar. Citrus essential oils (lemon and orange) shouldn't be used on your face or body because they can make your skin more sensitive to the sun.

Try: Peppermint for a cooling effect or rosemary for when you're feeling run down and need a pick-me-up.

FRAGRANT ROOM SPRAYS

Create a room spray or linen spray by adding 15 drops of essential oil to a 3-oz. glass spray bottle. Add 1 teaspoon of witch hazel and top with distilled water. Shake before each use.

Try: 5 drops of lavender and 10 drops of Roman chamomile essential oil will create a calming blend that you can spray onto your sheets before bed, or try lemon essential oil for a room spray that could perk you up in the mornings.

SMELLING SALTS

Fill a small, lidded glass jar with coarse sea salt or Epsom salt. Add about 30 drops of essential oil per ounce of salt. When you need a boost, waft the smell toward your nose while breathing in. Replace the lid after each use.

Try: Cinnamon if you need to focus on homework or a test, jasmine for an energy boost, or vanilla when you'd like to calm down.

"IT IS NEVER TOO LATE TO BE WHAT YOU MIGHT HAVE BEEN."
— GEORGE ELIOT

Challenge Yourself

When you take on a challenge, be it a crossword puzzle or an intermediate climbing wall, you build confidence. Overcoming challenges can also help you build your self-esteem. Someone with high self-esteem knows they might fail at something — and they're OK with it. On the next page, you'll find some ways to challenge yourself.

- SAY HI TO A STRANGER.

- TACKLE A HUGE JIGSAW PUZZLE.

- ASK A FRIEND TO TEACH YOU HIS OR HER FAVORITE SPORT.

- MAKE A NEW RECIPE.

- LEARN FIVE PHRASES IN A NEW LANGUAGE.

- DO AS MANY PUSH-UPS AS YOU CAN.

- ONLY SAY POSITIVE THINGS FOR THE REST OF THE DAY. (NO COMPLAINTS!)

- MAKE EYE CONTACT WITH A STRANGER.

- PERFORM A POEM OR SONG IN FRONT OF A GROUP.

- TAKE A COLD SHOWER.

- FINISH A SUDOKU PUZZLE.

- TEACH YOURSELF TO PLAY A SONG ON THE PIANO.

- RAISE YOUR HAND WHEN SOMEONE ASKS FOR A VOLUNTEER.

- START UP A CONVERSATION WITH A STRANGER.

- TAKE THE STAIRS INSTEAD OF THE ESCALATOR.

- CALL UP AN OLD FRIEND JUST TO SAY HI.

- GIVE SOMEONE A COMPLIMENT.

- EAT SOMETHING YOU'VE NEVER TRIED BEFORE.

- DON'T SPEND ANY MONEY FOR AN ENTIRE DAY.

- ASK YOUR FRIENDS TO WRITE DOWN YOUR BEST QUALITIES.

DO SOMETHING YOU WERE ALWAYS AFRAID TO DO.

That's right: it's time to face a fear. Public speaking? Heights? Asking out someone you have a crush on? With a little bit of preparation and practice, you can do anything.

TRY SOMETHING YOU'VE FAILED AT BEFORE.

Is there something you've never been good at? Maybe it's drawing a face, baking cookies, or doing a cartwheel. Give it a second shot. Learn from your past mistakes – how can you improve them this time around?

MAKE YOURSELF VULNERABLE.

Sign up for an improvisation class, submit your poetry to a magazine, or audition for the school talent show. Whether it's a chance to embarrass yourself, bare your soul, or get some unwanted attention, the fear and excitement that comes with vulnerability can make you feel alive!

Body Scan

The body scan is a mindfulness practice that you can do anytime you have 20 minutes or so. It's important to take your time doing it, spending several minutes on each body part, so that you can really notice physical sensations. When we notice physical sensations, we are "in the present moment," which means that we're not worrying about the future or dwelling on something that happened in the past. Because of this, we feel less stressed!

- You begin by lying down on your back, gently resting your arms by your sides about six inches away from your body. You are allowing your legs to simply rest on the floor, noticing your whole body lying here resting.

- Now, turning your attention to your breath, you are seeing if you can simply notice your breath moving gently in and out of your body. You are noticing your belly rising and falling with each in-breath and each out-breath.

- Taking your time, you are shifting your attention from the belly down through to the soles of your feet. You are noticing any sensations you might be feeling. Maybe warmth or coolness? Tingling or tickling?

- After several minutes of noticing sensations, you are shifting your attention to the rest of your feet. You are noticing what sensations are in your toes or heels — maybe pleasure, maybe pain, or maybe nothing at all. Whatever you are feeling, it is perfectly OK. You're just noticing what's there, not trying to create any feelings that aren't there. If you notice any discomfort, see if you can explore the experience with curiosity. You are asking yourself, "What is this sensation I'm feeling? What's it like?"

- As you inhale, you are moving your attention from the feet up into the ankles, first on one foot and then the next. You are noticing any sensations that might be in your ankles. Then you are slowly moving to your calves, noticing sensations on the skin of your calves, perhaps feeling the texture of your clothing. Is it smooth? Rough? Scratchy? You are simply observing any sensations that are there, letting them be just as they are.

- When you notice your mind has wandered, as it will, simply return to the sensations in your body. Don't worry about it, or judge yourself for it. This is what our minds do naturally.

- After a minute or two, you are shifting attention to your knees. You are noticing sensations that are at the front of your knees, and the sides, and the area behind your knees. You are taking your time, spending several minutes here. You are just observing with curiosity.

- Now you are shifting your attention to your thighs. What's here? Are your muscles relaxed? What does the sensation of clothing feel like? What does the feeling of contact with the floor or bed feel like beneath your thighs? Is there pressure there? Perhaps discomfort? Or do you notice a softness and warmth? You are remembering that there's no right or wrong way to feel.

- You are shifting your awareness now to your belly. You are focusing on your breathing and the feeling of your belly expanding and contracting with each breath, gently moving, almost like a boat rocking on the sea.

- After a few minutes, you are shifting your attention to your chest. You are noticing your chest rising and falling — a gentle movement with each breath. Perhaps you are even hearing your heart beating. You are taking a few minutes here to simply notice sensations.

- You are shifting your attention now down both arms to the tips of your fingers on both hands, noticing anything that you're feeling there. What are you feeling on the tips of your fingers? Any sensations at all? Moving now to the palms of your hands, what do you notice here? Maybe warmth? Coolness? A sense of moisture or dryness? Perhaps a pulsing? You are spending a few minutes here, just noticing.

· Now you are moving to the tops of your hands. What's the temperature here like? Is it different from the palms of your hands? Are there any different sensations here?

· Moving up through your wrists and forearms, you are noticing any feelings along your lower arms and upper arms. You are allowing the sensations to be just as they are. You are seeing if there's any tightness in your shoulders or upper back — this is a place people often keep their tension.

· Now, moving to your neck and throat, what sensations are you noticing on your neck? This is another place where many people hold tension and stress. Do you notice any tightness here or feelings of discomfort?

· After a few minutes, you are slowly shifting attention to your head and face, checking in with the muscles in your forehead and cheeks. Are these muscles relaxed or tight? Do you notice any sensations in your eye sockets or other areas around your eyes?

· Now you are letting go of sensations in your head and face, bringing your attention back to your breath. You are noticing your belly expanding and contracting slowly with each breath.

· Taking your time and only when you feel ready, you are gently opening your eyes, stretching your body, turning to your right, and sitting up.

Notice how you feel after doing this body scan. Do you feel different from the way you felt before?

Pamper Yourself

If you're feeling run down, overworked, or stressed out, a little pampering can boost your mood and calm you down. These recipes are a treat for your feet. The peppermint and tea tree essential oils cause a cooling, tingling effect, but they may also put some pep in your step — peppermint is said to be energizing.

Tingly Foot Scrub

YOU WILL NEED:

1 cup sea salt
½ cup olive oil
12 drops peppermint essential oil
12 drops tea tree essential oil

After a good massage with this invigorating scrub, your feet will feel soft and smooth.

Directions:

Mix all ingredients in a small bowl.

To use, massage a handful onto your feet while sitting over a bathtub or a large bowl of water with a towel underneath it. Rinse, then pat feet dry with a clean towel. Scoop any extra scrub into a lidded glass container. Store in a cool, dry place. Use within 3-4 weeks.

Be careful! Oils and butters can make bathtub surfaces slippery. A non-slip bath mat may help. Wipe bathtub floor with a dry towel when finished.

YOU WILL NEED:

1 cup baking soda
½ cup Epsom salts
10 drops peppermint essential oil

Foot Soak for Tired Toes

Bring your feet back to life after a long day with this energizing soak.

Directions:

Mix all ingredients in a bowl.

To use, fill a large bowl (big enough to fit both your feet) halfway with warm water. Pour ½ cup of the mixture into the large bowl and store the rest in a lidded glass container. Let your feet soak for 10-15 minutes, then pat dry with a clean towel. Discard the liquid in the sink.

Get Some Sleep

When you get a good night's sleep, you'll wake up feeling energized and ready to take on the day.

Sleeping DOs

1. EXERCISE

Work out each day, and you'll be more likely to fall asleep at night. Exercising earlier in the day is better. Breaking a sweat late at night can keep you up for hours.

2. CHAMOMILE TEA

Chamomile tea is caffeine free and is said to help induce sleep. A warm glass of milk can do the trick too. Just don't drink too many liquids before bed. One glass provides all the soothing you need.

3. BREATHING

You should be able to fall asleep within 15 minutes of lying in bed. Breathing can help make that happen. Try the Equal Breathing or Relaxing Breath exercises from page 21 to help send you to dreamland.

4. SCHEDULE

Your bedtime and wake-up call should be the same time every day, even on the weekends. Sticking to a schedule helps train your internal clock. Before you know it, you'll be hopping out of bed one minute before your alarm goes off.

5. HIDE THE CLOCK

If you can't fall asleep, the worst thing you can do is stare at the clock. It will only stress you out more and make it even harder to fall asleep. Stop that vicious cycle before it starts and don't keep a clock by your bed. If you use your phone as an alarm, turn it upside down and keep it out of reach.

Sleeping DON'Ts

1. TV

Many people like falling asleep with the TV on or watching their favorite show right before bed. But the light and noise aren't good for those who are trying to catch some ZZZs. Even if you fall asleep quickly, it will take you longer to reach the quality sleep zone, or REM stage, which means you'll wake up drowsy.

2. PHONE

Is your phone the last thing you check each night and the first thing you check each morning? That's not good! While it's fun to browse social media feeds in bed, phones emit blue light, which messes up your internal body clock.

3. NAPS

Long naps can alter your sleep patterns. If you really need an afternoon snooze, keep it to a 20-minute catnap.

4. CAFFEINE

Caffeine is a stimulant that begins to slowly wear down within a few hours, but it can stay in your body for eight hours or more. That means you should avoid caffeine after lunch or it could disrupt your sleeping patterns at night.

5. HOMEWORK IN BED

Don't bring your homework or your laptop to bed. Save it for the desk or dining room table — otherwise you'll find yourself stressed out in bed, which definitely won't help you fall asleep.

"DREAMING, AFTER ALL, IS A FORM OF PLANNING." – GLORIA STEINEM

The 60-Minute Wind-Down

1 HOUR BEFORE BEDTIME . . .

Take five minutes to wrap up any conversations, homework, or TV shows. Now turn off all screens. The light from bright screens signals to the brain to stop producing melatonin, a hormone which helps promote sleep. But falling asleep is exactly what you're trying to do!

55 MINUTES BEFORE BEDTIME . . .

Pick out your clothes for tomorrow, make your lunch, or pack your bag. Simple routines like this — when they are repeated every night — can send signals to your brain that it's almost time to sleep.

40 MINUTES BEFORE BEDTIME . . .

At night, our body temperature drops a bit. Take a warm bath for 15 minutes. When you get out of the tub, your body will cool down quickly and send a signal to your brain that it's time for bed. For an extra treat, add the bath salts from page 59.

25 MINUTES BEFORE BEDTIME . . .

Dim the lights. The easiest way to regulate your sleep cycle is through light. If you don't have a dimmer, think about switching out the light bulbs in your lamps with ones that have a softer glow (look for lower wattage and less lumens).

24 MINUTES BEFORE BEDTIME . . .

Stretch lightly for a few minutes. Try the Wide-Legged Forward Bend (page 13) and the Legs Up the Wall Pose (page 17). End with Corpse Pose (page 19).

20 MINUTES BEFORE BEDTIME . . .

Hop into bed. Make sure you're comfortable and cozy. Put on a pair of socks if your feet are too cold. Pick up your favorite book or write in your journal for the next 15 minutes.

5 MINUTES BEFORE BEDTIME . . .

Put away your book or journal and shut off the lights completely. Try the Relaxing Breath from page 21, which naturally helps you fall asleep quickly.

BEDTIME . . . ZZZ . . .

The majority of teens don't get enough sleep. Without a good night's rest, you may have trouble concentrating, learning, listening, and more. Sleeping in on the weekends isn't the answer. There's no such thing as "catching up." If you want to wake up feeling energized, you need to prioritize sleep and stick to a schedule, which means getting up and going to bed the same time every day.

Find Your Balance

All these projects are great for getting immediate results, but what about longer-term issues you're dealing with? Check out the following pages for advice on time management, making decisions, learning to speak up for yourself, and more. While they may take time, there are always things we can improve about ourselves. The following pages are a great place to start.

IF YOU HAVE TROUBLE SPEAKING UP FOR YOURSELF . . . CHECK OUT THE ADVICE ON PAGE 143.

IF YOU'RE OVERWHELMED BY A BUSY SCHEDULE . . . GET HELP MANAGING YOUR TIME WITH THE TIPS ON PAGE 144.

IF YOU CAN'T MAKE A DECISION . . . READ THE STEPS FOR DECISION-MAKING ON PAGE 146.

IF YOU FIND YOURSELF PROCRASTINATING REGULARLY . . . FOLLOW THE GAMIFYING TIPS ON PAGE 148 TO HELP YOU BECOME MORE PRODUCTIVE.

IF YOU'RE ALWAYS COMPARING YOURSELF TO OTHERS . . . GET STARTED FOCUSING ON YOURSELF BY FOLLOWING THE ADVICE ON PAGE 150.

Speak Up

These exercises can help you feel more confident and be more assertive.

SPEAK SLOWLY.

Don't rush through the conversation, otherwise you'll sound nervous. It's OK to pause occasionally and think about what you want to say before you say it.

SPEAK FIRMLY.

Be assertive, not aggressive.

SPEAK CLEARLY.

Don't speak so quietly that no one can hear you.

MAKE EYE CONTACT.

Don't look at the floor. Strong eye contact can be difficult, but it's one of the most important ways to connect with an audience.

WORK ON YOUR POSTURE.

Body language says a lot. Stand up straight and let your arms rest gently at your sides. Turn to page 122 for tips on how to sit or stand correctly.

DON'T FORGET TO BREATHE.

Slow, deep breaths can help you remain calm and can help keep your voice steady as you speak.

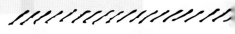

Manage Your Time

Fitting school, fun, family, friends, and sports or other activities into one day can seem impossible. But with a plan, each day will become much more manageable, and you may even feel more productive. These time management tips can keep you motivated, on schedule, and may even create some room in your schedule for a relaxing break!

PRIORITIZE

To-do lists are great, but when they're 15 items long, it's very unlikely you'll get to everything by the end of the day. Instead of making the world's longest to-do list, choose the three most important things that have to be completed each day, and make sure you accomplish those tasks.

BREAK IT DOWN

If you have an overwhelming project due next month or a big goal you'd like to reach, break it into chunks. How can a project or goal be separated into smaller milestones? Set deadlines for each portion of your project or goal and write down the timeline into your planner or your calendar. For example, if you have a presentation due in history class in three weeks, break it into three portions. Week one: gather notes and draft an outline of your presentation. Week two: begin working on your slideshow or poster and picking out the most important information to include. Week three: practice your oral presentation and make your visual presentation look clean and professional.

SET BOUNDARIES

One of the reasons why it's hard to be productive is because we are constantly trying to multitask. If you need to spend an hour doing homework, do it fully and without apology. Shut off your phone and computer, close your bedroom door, and don't let anything break your focus. If you are prioritizing family time this week and need to miss a friend's party for your grandpa's birthday, be upfront. You can make time for your friends another weekend.

REMOVE WHAT YOU CAN

It's easy to overcommit. Ask yourself: what can wait? What can you say no to? Maybe your laundry can wait until Saturday or that movie you promised your sister you'd go to can wait until next weekend. Finding balance is important, but so is being realistic with what you need to do and how you're going to do it.

FOCUS ON THE BIG PICTURE

If you're a perfectionist, you may be wasting precious time obsessing over the details. Sometimes "good enough" is great! Don't be so hard on yourself. Give yourself permission to *not* go above and beyond every time.

"ALWAYS TRY TO GET BETTER EVERY TIME YOU DO SOMETHING. YOU DON'T HAVE TO GET IT PERFECT EVERY TIME." – JENNIE CHEN

Make a Decision

Hit the snooze button or get up? Bagel or eggs for breakfast? These pants or that skirt? Walk or take the bus? Blue or black pen? Every day, you probably make a ton of decisions before the first school bell rings. Sometimes even those little decisions can turn into lengthy internal debates, which can be frustrating.

Major decisions can really wear on you — and on your emotions. The decision-making process is stressful, which makes it hard to think clearly and confidently. Think of a difficult decision you need to make later today or this week. Then try one of these strategies to help you settle on an answer.

When you have to make a choice between two or more things, create a list of criteria that are important to you, then see how many each choice meets.

SET A TIME LIMIT.

Self-imposed deadlines can work for big or small decisions. When you're working against the clock, you'll have to limit the amount of debating, research, and people you talk to for advice. You'll have to eventually go with your gut.

Example: "We'll spend five minutes deciding which movie to watch," or "I'll ask three people for advice on whether or not I should try out for the track team."

MAKE A PRO-CON LIST.

Pro-con lists are especially effective for yes/no questions. To make one, divide a piece of notebook paper into two halves: one for pros and one for cons. Assign one point to each pro and each con. Add up your totals and make a decision based on the results.

Example: "I should join the track team because even though I'll have less free time, I'll make new friends, get in shape, and challenge myself."

LIMIT THE NUMBER OF CHOICES.

Let's say you need to choose a paint color for your room and you have 10 different shades of purple. News flash! You'll never be able to decide. Some of us get so hung up at finding the "best" option that it stops us from making progress. If you have too many choices, quickly reduce the number of options to two or three.

Example: "Let's make this easier: The Freeze or Julie Ann's for ice cream?"

PRETEND YOU'RE GIVING ADVICE TO A FRIEND.

Try to look at the situation from an outside perspective. If a friend came to you asking for advice, what would you tell him or her? If you can separate the decision from your emotions for a few minutes, you might realize there was an obvious choice all along or that you were overlooking some important details.

Example: "When I look at this from an outsider's point of view, I know that I should go because it would be a good experience for me."

CHOOSE YOUR BATTLES.

Is there someone else involved in the decision-making process? Maybe you should just leave it up to them. If you always fight with your siblings about which movie to watch, you could let your brother choose this one — as long as you get to choose next time.

Example: "I'll let you decide where we eat lunch today, as long as we go to my favorite pizza place next week."

FLIP A COIN.

For smaller decisions, sometimes it's best to leave it up to chance. Assign one outcome to "heads" and one outcome to "tails." Flip the coin in the air and let it land on the ground. Whatever side is facing up is the decision you'll go with.

Example: "Heads means I wear the black shirt, tails means I wear the blue one."

"GO CONFIDENTLY IN THE DIRECTION OF YOUR DREAMS AND LIVE THE LIFE YOU HAVE IMAGINED." – HENRY DAVID THOREAU

Be Productive

"Gamifying" is a mental trick. It turns a task into a game by using motivators like competition, rewards, or time limits. The more you "win," the more you'll want to keep winning . . . and the more productive you'll become. These tricks will help you finish something that you've been avoiding — from an English paper to violin practice to cleaning your room.

Here's one way to stay motivated: if you don't complete the task, you have to delete your favorite apps from your phone. You can always add them back!

SPRINT!

Set a timer for 30 minutes — and work the entire time. Push distractions to the side. When the buzzer rings, take a five- or ten-minute break. Then get back at it! Breaking your task into a more manageable workload can keep you motivated throughout the process.

SET RULES

Get strict with yourself. Make your desk a phone-free zone. Disable the Wi-Fi on your computer when you're working on an English paper. Set a "no social media after 8 p.m." rule. Whatever it takes to keep you focused! If you break a rule, take away something for a night like your favorite TV show or app.

CHUNK

"Chunking" is all about grouping similar tasks together, which makes it easier to focus. When you're more focused, you're more efficient. Can you group all of your reading and note-taking into one night this week? Can you finish writing those two papers in one session? Can you complete all of this week's chores in one afternoon?

MAKE A BET

An accountability partner is someone who checks in on your progress and holds you to your goals. You could partner up with someone for the whole school year and offer each other a little friendly competition. Or simply tell a parent "I'm going to finish this geometry assignment by 8 p.m." Getting another person involved might be the motivation you need.

DANGLE A CARROT

Promise yourself a treat if you complete a certain task or goal. For example, if I get my homework done before 8 p.m., I can watch my favorite TV show. Or, if I get my paper done, I can turn my phone back on.

DON'T BREAK THE CHAIN

Keep track of your productivity on a chart. On a horizontal axis, write the days of the week. On the vertical axis, write this week's daily goals. For example, complete my homework by 9 p.m., stop using social media after 8 p.m., get 9 hours of sleep, work on my presentation for 30 minutes, etc. When you meet a goal, shade in that box for that day.

MASTER THE TO-DO LIST

A to-do list is motivating because it feels great when you get to cross something off. But if your to-do list is too long, you'll never get that satisfaction! Instead, try creating more than one list — such as a daily and a weekly version. The weekly list keeps you organized while the daily list can help you focus on three things to complete each day. Or try making two to-do lists for the week: one for your personal life and one for school. The visual separation will help you feel less overwhelmed. If you're feeling burned out as you chip away at your school list, move to the personal list — or vice versa. Make it fun by giving yourself a point for each item you complete.

UNDERSTAND YOUR HABITS

Being productive means getting tasks done quickly and efficiently. In order to do this, you'll have to pay attention to your habits. Track your progress for one week and keep notes. How long did it take to do your homework every night? Why do you keep getting distracted? Why did it take so long for you to start? When do you feel most creative and energized?

Stop Comparing

When you stop comparing yourself to others, you make yourself happier! Studies have found that self-acceptance is a key element of happiness. That means you accept all the things that make you who you are, knowing that your areas to strengthen are part of what make you human — and what make you interesting. So how do you stop comparing and start loving yourself?

If your social media feeds are making you feel depressed or anxious, delete your account! Or log out for a week and see if you feel any better. See the technology detox tips on page 48 for more ideas.

Mindfulness Tip: Remember that we are all imperfect, because we are all human. Our "imperfections" are what make us who we are.

1. MAKE A LIST OF TEN THINGS THAT MAKE YOU *YOU.*

Writer and director Joss Whedon once said, "Whatever makes you weird is probably your greatest asset." Different is interesting. Whether you're quiet and shy or loud and funny, embrace these qualities. Celebrate yourself!

2. JOT DOWN TEN THINGS YOU WOULD LIKE TO ACHIEVE.

Someone else's path might not be your path, even if it looks perfect from the outside. Any time spent focusing on others is time not spent on yourself. Whatever triggered a jealous response in you is a sign — it signals what you want in your life. Instead of getting depressed about what's missing from your life, look at it as motivation to help you reach your dreams.

3. WRITE DOWN TEN THINGS YOU COULD WORK ON.

Get to know yourself! Instead of avoiding the things you need to work on — like your tendency to procrastinate on homework — acknowledge them and remember that it's OK not to be perfect. In fact, none of us is. Write down ten areas you could strengthen. Think about why they are a challenge for you and what you can do to improve these behaviors. Use a kind voice to gently encourage yourself to do your best. Ask a friend or family member for advice.

4. DOCUMENT TEN OF YOUR BIGGEST ACHIEVEMENTS.

So, a friend had something great happen to them lately. It doesn't make all the great things you've done less than. They're still great too! If a friend is smart, it doesn't make you less smart. You can *both* be smart. Being grateful for all the amazing things happening in your life right now will bring you joy. And cheer on others when they have their moment.

> "DON'T COMPARE YOURSELF TO OTHERS. COMPARE YOURSELF
> TO THE PERSON YOU WERE YESTERDAY." – ANONYMOUS

What Does Stress Do to Your Body?

Let's say you're stressed out before a big game. Just before it starts, you get an adrenaline rush that pushes you to focus and gives you a burst of energy. That kind of stress can be good.

But chronic stress — stress that lasts for hours, days, or weeks — is harmful. In fact, many health organizations say stress is the number-one public health threat.

There is a difference between feeling temporarily bummed out and feeling depressed for weeks on end. If you're experiencing a continued feeling of hopelessness and a constant lack of motivation, you should get help. Turn to page 154 for more information.

Your Body Under Stress

1. STRESS CAN MAKE YOU GRUMPY OR SAD.

When you're stressed out, you may feel forgetful or distracted, as well as anxious and irritable. Prolonged stress can make it harder to sleep, eat, and function normally — and that's no fun.

2. STRESS MAY MAKE YOU SICK AND SLUGGISH.

Stress can make you more likely to get sick or catch a cold, and then make it harder for you to get rid of an illness once it strikes. Stress can also affect your appetite, which may lead to junk food cravings or skipping meals — both of which will make you feel tired.

3. STRESS CAN MAKE IT DIFFICULT TO FOCUS.

Stress triggers the "fight or flight response" in your body. This is helpful when you're in physical danger — your body and your brain think and react quickly when there is a threat. Your body will eventually return to the way it was before you became stressed — unless you're constantly stressed out. Chronic stress can make your body think you're constantly in danger, even if you're not.

4. STRESS CAN MAKE IT HARDER TO REMEMBER.

A part of the brain called the hippocampus is responsible for learning and memory. The hippocampus becomes dampened when your emotions are heightened, which often happens when you're stressed. That means you could have difficulty learning and remembering facts in class or important events such as a loved one's birthday.

5. STRESS CAN REDUCE GRAY MATTER IN YOUR BRAIN.

Gray matter processes information in your brain, but stress causes changes to the brain. These changes affect your ability to do things like regulate emotions and make decisions. When your brain structure is damaged, not only may it be more difficult to concentrate, but it may also become more difficult to deal with stress in the future.

Your Body Relaxed

1. RELAXATION CAN PUT YOU IN A GOOD MOOD.

When you're calm, your brain can regulate your emotions better. That means you're less likely to get irritated or angry about small annoyances, such as your younger sister borrowing a pair of jeans without your permission.

2. RELAXATION CAN MAKE YOUR BODY STRONGER.

You body is designed to handle stress, but chronic stress is not good for you. When you're stressed, your muscles may tense up, your heart may beat faster, and you may even get a stomachache. Relaxation techniques not only help you feel better but can also fight off colds and reduce acne and other skin conditions.

3. RELAXATION CAN HELP YOU THINK MORE CLEARLY.

With a calm mind, you're able to make decisions more clearly and quickly instead of feeling flustered and overwhelmed.

4. RELAXATION CAN IMPROVE YOUR MEMORY.

When you're not stressed out, you may be able to recall and remember things without trying too hard. You're less likely to forget your keys when you walk out the door, and you may even perform better on your next test. That's because there's a link between cortisol, the stress hormone, and retaining new information. A certain amount of stress is good for you, but too much is not.

5. MEDITATION CAN CHANGE THE STRUCTURE OF THE BRAIN — FOR THE BETTER.

Research has shown that meditation can increase gray matter in certain areas of your brain. How cool is that? That means it's possible that the damage caused by chronic stress could be repaired over time. Turn to page 8 to learn more about meditation.

Do You Need Help?

If you've ever thought about harming yourself or others, seek help right away. Turn to page 157 for a list of resources.

The exercises and ideas in this book offer help for short-term stress. They are not cures or treatments for more serious, long-term issues, such as chronic depression, suicidal thoughts, self-harming behavior, disordered eating, addiction, post-traumatic stress disorder, and generalized anxiety disorder.

Symptoms of more serious mental health issues, such as depression or anxiety, can include any or all of the following:

- LETHARGY AND/OR FATIGUE
- RESTLESSNESS
- FEELINGS OF GUILT
- TROUBLE SLEEPING, INCLUDING OVERSLEEPING, INSOMNIA, AND RESTLESS SLEEP
- LACK OF STRENGTH OR ENERGY
- LACK OF INTEREST IN DAILY ACTIVITIES AND HOBBIES
- CHANGES IN APPETITE
- WEIGHT GAIN OR WEIGHT LOSS
- DIFFICULTY CONCENTRATING, MAKING DECISIONS, AND REMEMBERING
- LACK OF SELF-CONFIDENCE
- PERSISTENT FEELING OF SADNESS
- FEELING AS THOUGH YOUR LIFE ISN'T WORTH LIVING
- PERSISTENT PHYSICAL SYMPTOMS IN RESPONSE TO YOUR EMOTIONS (SUCH AS GETTING A HEADACHE OR STOMACHACHE AS A RESULT OF SADNESS OR ANXIETY)

- THOUGHTS OF DEATH OR SUICIDE
- MOOD SWINGS
- SOCIAL ISOLATION OR PERSISTENT FEELINGS OF LONELINESS
- CHANGE IN ENERGY LEVEL
- CHANGE IN SELF-ESTEEM
- FEELING EASILY OR OVERLY IRRITABLE
- FEELINGS OF HOPELESSNESS AND PESSIMISM
- APATHY
- EXCESSIVE CRYING
- SIGNIFICANT CHANGES IN DAILY BEHAVIOR
- LACK OF MOTIVATION
- FEELING "EMPTY"
- SLOWNESS OF ACTIVITY
- RACING THOUGHTS AND/OR EXCESSIVE WORRY
- FEELING A SENSE OF IMPENDING DANGER
- EXCESSIVE SWEATING, TREMBLING, OR SHORTNESS OF BREATH

If any of these negative feelings have been affecting you regularly for two weeks or more, you may need some extra attention. It's important to seek help as soon as possible, especially if your symptoms are affecting your relationships, your health and well-being, or your ability to fulfill your responsibilities.

How to Ask for Help

If you or a friend needs help, there are many people and resources you can turn to. A doctor, social worker, or school counselor can offer professional help. If you need help figuring out how to contact one of these people, reach out to a trusted friend, family member, or teacher.

On a day-to-day basis, friends and family members can keep you on track. Don't forget: asking for help makes you stronger, not weaker.

In addition to seeking out professional help, you can ask supportive, reliable, confident friends and family members to . . .

HELP YOU STAY POSITIVE.

LISTEN WHEN YOU NEED SOMEONE TO TALK TO.

HELP YOU CREATE AND MANAGE A SCHEDULE.

REMIND YOU THAT OTHER PEOPLE STRUGGLE TOO.

MOTIVATE YOU TO FINISH YOUR HOMEWORK ON TIME.

MAKE YOU LAUGH.

HELP YOU GET YOUR CHORES DONE.

PRAISE YOUR PROGRESS.

REMIND YOU THAT YOU WILL FEEL BETTER SOMEDAY.

WAKE YOU UP ON TIME — NO SNOOZE BUTTONS ALLOWED.

GO FOR A WALK WITH YOU.

MAKE DOCTOR APPOINTMENTS FOR YOU.

GIVE YOU PEP TALKS AND TELL YOU WHY YOU'RE GREAT.

WHO CAN HELP

National Suicide Prevention Lifeline
www.sptsusa.org
1-800-273-TALK (8255)

Substance Abuse and Mental Health Services Administration's National Helpline
www.samhsa.gov
1-800-662-HELP (4357)

National Eating Disorders Association
www.nationaleatingdisorders.org
Crisis text line: text "NEDA" to 741741
1-800-931-2237

S.A.F.E. Alternatives
www.selfinjury.com
1-800-DONT-CUT (366-8288)

Gay, Lesbian, Bisexual and Transgender National Hotline
www.glnh.org
1-888-THE-GLNH (843-4564)

The National Center for Grieving Children & Families
www.dougy.org
1-866-775-5683

National Runaway Safeline
www.1800runaway.org
1-800-RUNAWAY (786-2929)

Planned Parenthood
www.plannedparenthood.org/info-for-teens
1-800-230-PLAN (7526)

National Sexual Assault Hotline
www.rainn.org
1-800-656-HOPE (4673)

National Domestic Violence Hotline
www.thehotline.org
1-800-799-SAFE (7233)

National Alliance on Mental Illness
www.nami.org
1-800-950-6264

Aubre Andrus is an award-winning children's book author with books published by Scholastic, American Girl, and more. She cherishes her time spent as the Lifestyle Editor of *American Girl* magazine where she developed crafts, recipes, and party ideas for girls. When she's not writing, Aubre loves traveling around the world, and some of her favorite places include India, Cambodia, and Japan. She currently lives in Los Angeles with her husband. You can find her website at www.aubreandrus.com.

A mindfulness practitioner for almost 40 years and a lifelong educator, Dr. Karen Bluth is faculty at University of North Carolina at Chapel Hill, where her research focuses on the roles that self-compassion and mindfulness play in promoting well-being in youth. She is author of *The Self-Compassion Workbook for Teens* (New Harbinger Publishers) and co-creator of the curriculum *Making Friends with Yourself: A Mindful Self-Compassion Program for Teens*.